ARISE
and
SHINE

AWAKEN TO A FRESH PERSPECTIVE

KENNETH BONNER SR.

Published by Emerge Editing Group.
ISBN: 979-8-89412-464-3
Printed in The United States of America
Book Cover Design-
Interior Design-Emerge Editing Group.
Copy Editor: Daphney M. Chaney
For ordering information contact:
Kbonner34@gmail.com
www.kennethbonnersr.com

DEDICATION

This book is dedicated to: Everyone longing for a better life. I am deeply thankful to God for this wonderful opportunity to share the invaluable tools I have learned by overcoming life's trials. My heart is filled with gratitude for my wife, children, family, and friends who have consistently provided prayer and unwavering support for me and my journey with Christ Jesus. I am humbled that God trusted me to deliver this message of hope, inspiration, and empowerment through the Word of God. I am grateful for my Lord Jesus Christ, without whom I would be nothing.

To my wife: Your unconditional love, caring heart, unwavering encouragement and persistent push has guided me to fulfill my calling and complete what I started. You are an incredible source of motivation and love! Thank you for who you are and who you are to me. You support my dreams and the vision God has given me. God has a purpose for us, and I see it every day. I love you!

WHAT PEOPLE ARE SAYING ABOUT THIS BOOK:

Another opportunity to get a different perspective on life's journey. A series of messages that help create a balance of understanding. Makes you sit back and analyze who you are, what you are, and what you are trying to be. Life is hard and it has its challenges but with the right insight and understanding of purpose, the course of life can be navigated towards a brighter future. Kenneth helps with that insight, spiritual discernment, and passion in his writings. There is something on every page that can help you through your day. Another great piece of work by Kenneth Bonner.

-Reggie Smith, author of
Beyond Blood, and Mental
Health Advocate.

If you are looking for a great read that's fascinating, thought-provoking, and something that will force you to rethink areas in your life where you might seem defeated. Look no further, because this is the book that will challenge your mind and your thought process to develop a different perspective on how you are already victorious over anything you have gone through or maybe in the process of life simply lifting. This book is an absolute page turner that will have you wanting to continue to read it without putting the book down. Be ready to take notes because the Gems dropped just from the first chapter will have you wanting to just sit, reflect, and then apply all that is being taught through real life experiences. Are you ready to see your life through a different lens? I can tell you by the time you put it down, you will not only have discovered a new you, but you will also experience growth, healing, and restoration as you navigate this season in your life. Arise and shine people and go pick up this book today you will not be disappointed.

-Jacqueline Wells,
B.A. Business Administration

ACKNOWLEDGMENTS

First and foremost, I want to acknowledge my Lord and Savior, Jesus Christ. He was the first to love me and believe in me. I do not take the grace given to me lightly, for He could have chosen another to carry out this mission.

I would like to extend a special thanks to my publisher and editor, Daphney Chaney, for helping me finish this project. Trusting people with your work is difficult and even harder to get them to see your vision. Thank you for listening to the Holy Spirit and pulling more out of me to ensure this project accomplishes God's purpose.

I am grateful for my children, who are my constant motivators. Their passion and drive encourage me daily to persevere in life. They are my reason why.

My mother, an amazing mom, who selflessly sacrificed her own aspirations to care for her children, has been a profound inspiration. Her commitment and devotion to the Lord have taught me to keep Him first in all aspects of life. She is the reason I am dedicated to the Lord Jesus.

To my late Father, who may no longer be with us in body but resides eternally in my heart, I am thankful for instilling in me the values of always striving for excellence and treating others right. I miss and love you!

My sisters, Sherrie and Diana. You both have been a tremendous source of inspiration to me. Your unwavering determination to pursue your goals and your sincere desire to see me thrive are invaluable to me. You are my inspiration.

To my brothers, John and Marcus, I want to express my love for both of you.

My brother-in-law Reggie, I sincerely appreciate your authenticity and the trust I can place in our conversations without fear of judgment. Your support means the world to me, bro!

To my Stepmom and my late stepbrothers. I love you all and miss you dearly!

To my numerous aunts, uncles, cousins, nieces, and nephews, you have all been a tremendous blessing and a continuous source of encouragement throughout my life. My cousins are like dear sisters and brothers to me. While there are too many of you to name individually, please understand that each of you hold a cherished and unique place in my heart.

I wish to express my gratitude to my uncle, Bishop Fred Jackson, for his unwavering belief in me and for imparting reverence for God.

To Jessie L. Morgan (RIH) and Linda Morgan, Jay and Jennifer Peikert, Carlton and Deborah Edwards, Pam and Kelly Hughes, Ashley and Timothy Twigg your impact on my life is immeasurable, and I will forever be thankful. Thank you for allowing God to work through you and embracing me as a part of your kingdom family.

To my friends who are like my family, though too numerous to name individually, I am profoundly grateful for your recognition of my potential, faith in me, and support in my growth. I hold deep affection for all of you and treasure the relationships we have built. May God bless each of you abundantly, overflowing with the same kindness and support you have poured into my life.

CONTENTS

Introduction

Welcome to *Arise and Shine: Awaken to a New Perspective!* This book is a heartfelt journey through the trials and triumphs that have shaped my life. It is a testament to the transformative power of faith and the healing grace of Jesus Christ. I witnessed my parents' painful divorce and never imagined I would follow in their footsteps, experiencing not one but two divorces myself. I acknowledge my role in entering these marriages unhealed and unprepared. Instead of being united by God to fulfill His purposes, I sought to satisfy my desires to feel wanted, safe, and secure. Burdened by shame, guilt, and the sting of rejection from a young age, I grappled with my identity. These shadows of my past influenced my decisions. I lived under a cloud of shame from multiple divorces, financial hardships, and low self-worth —until God's light pierced through, illuminating my path and guiding me toward a brighter future.

To truly walk in His light, I had to learn the true meaning of surrender. This journey of surrender taught me total dependence upon God. As my faith deepened, so did my confidence in Him. This newfound confidence empowered me to release relationships that were no longer aligned with the

God-given purpose and the character I sought to embody in Christ. You will see how easily it is to stray from faith in God to idolatry. Our hearts can easily be deceived and filled with pride. God masters in reeling us back to Himself.

The transition to leave everything behind was not easy. It came with challenges—loneliness, tear-filled nights, and moments of doubt. Yet, in these trials, I found strength and resilience. I embraced the pain, knowing each struggle was a bridge toward a more meaningful transformation. In *"Arise and Shine,"* I share my story with transparency and vulnerability. I am open about my struggles, the deep wounds of my soul, and the pain that sent me deep into depression. I hope that through my story, you will see the incredible healing and transforming power of Jesus Christ. Each chapter of this book is designed to be more than just a testimony. You will find points to ponder, prayers to lift your spirit, and journal sections as you reflect inwardly and allow God to speak to you. These features were crafted to enhance your deep engagement with the material and enable you to apply the practical lessons to your life.

I pray that you will be filled with overflowing joy and peace as you journey through these pages. May you find the strength to triumph over your past failures, mistakes, and decisions. Let this book be a ray of hope, guiding you to arise and shine as you awaken to new perspectives. *Kenneth Bonner*

CHAPTER ONE
NAVIGATING LIFE'S FRUSTRATIONS

There have been numerous occasions when I felt like I was far from where I wanted to be and even farther from where I believed God intended me to be. These moments were marked by challenges, difficulties, and a deep sense of despair. I experienced a whirlwind of emotions and seemed incapable of finding peace, even if it had smacked me in the face. What made it worse was that these periods did not just wound my ego; they affected my heart and attitude, transforming me into an angry individual. I harbored anger towards God, though I never openly admitted it. I was also angry at myself and the circumstances in which I found myself.

It is challenging when you have dedicated your life to God and earnestly strive to live by His principles, yet it seems like you are not reaping the benefits. We often compare our lives with those of non-believers and wonder if it might be easier to live their way rather than the righteous path. It can feel as though they are thriving in every aspect of their lives, while some of us who follow Jesus Christ are struggling just to get by. This is a disheartening place to find oneself. It would make anyone angry. I have found myself in this place numerous times, only to realize that the areas where I struggled were those where I did not trust God enough. By that, I mean I had not genuinely surrendered those areas of my life to Him. I may have professed my belief in Him and claimed to trust Him, but my actions did not align with my words.

I prayed earnestly, and when God revealed that my lack of trust, belief, and faith was the root cause, I hesitated to accept this truth. However, eventually, I had no choice but to acknowledge it and confront it. It is never easy when the Lord corrects you, but it is an act of love (Hebrews 12:6). It is a painful realization when you are told you have been doing it wrong and that you lack the faith, trust, and belief necessary to change your circumstances. But it is also a blessing that God loves you enough to unveil these truths. Either He reveals them, or you keep spiraling without progress. I spent a while being angry with God and myself, feeling discouraged and disappointed. I had given my all to Him and adhered to His ways, yet He told me I was still falling short. Some of you reading this may be in that very place right now, or you may have been there. Let me tell you, it was a dark place for me to inhabit. I was not comfortable with the feedback God gave me about my life, but when I embraced the truth, everything began to change.

I was overwhelmed and frustrated, and on the brink of giving up, but I clung to reading the Holy Bible and earnestly praying. I asked God for help. I repeatedly told God that I surrendered to His will, but it was difficult for me to release my ingrained mindset. My intentions were pure, but my heart and mind remained far from what I confessed. After being inundated with countless opinions, thoughts, and ideologies, I struggled to accept that I was in this position because of my own choices. Something had to change! I started distancing myself from people and anything that hindered my progress. I immersed myself in God's Word more than ever before, inviting His presence through worship. I humbled myself and prayed. These actions were the keys to God transforming my situation. If I wanted to see change, I had to prioritize God. When I took these steps, it matured me and shifted my perspective on my relationship with God, my self-worth, and my life's direction. My perspective influenced my thoughts, and my thoughts guided my actions. I craved change and yearned for something different.

The roots of my behavior were jealousy and envy. It isn't easy for a man to admit that he struggled with low self-worth and felt the need to keep up appearances and compete with others. I had friends who had the things I wanted. They had wealth, luxury cars, nice clothes, and great careers. They were walking in their purpose and areas of giftedness also. I couldn't understand after surrendering my life to Christ, why hadn't doors of opportunity opened for me too? This took me back to the feelings of being unloved as a child. You will read in a few chapters how I measured my dad's love, or lack thereof, by the amount of money and gifts he'd give. This same behavior carried over into my adult years. The spirit of envy that bound me as a child also manifested in my adult years. I never showed it, but if they were discerning, then they knew I was envious. Whether they knew or not, it was my burden to bear. I knew that I needed to be delivered from the roots of envy and jealousy.

More men than you think or will admit also struggle with the same things. Many sit in church harboring resentment and/or angrily allow jealousy to build toward their pastors and other leaders who are in prominent positions. This often results from the attention shown by a plethora of women. Some men won't attend church because of the car the pastor drives. I'm not attempting to deflect by pointing out this grave issue. I want you to know that the man you love may still deal with intimidation, inferiority, rejection, and low self-worth. Some men are envious of their girlfriends and spouses' careers and anointing. There are also stories of men who have purposely tried to sabotage their spouse's careers and spiritual advancement. It is something that needs addressing.

OVERCOMING JEALOUSY AND ENVY

These spirits are rooted in pride. Although these words are used synonymously with one another, they are different. James 3:16 warns, "For where jealousy and selfish ambition exist, there will be disorder and every vile practice." The King James Version of the Bible uses the word "evil" instead of vile. Proverbs 14:30 says, "A heart at peace gives life to the body, but envy rots the bones." One of the Ten Commandments warns us about coveting. The Epistle of James tells us that covetous desires are born in the heart. He also tells us that we do not have what we ask for because we ask with the wrong or improper motives. When our heart's motivations for things are not right, we can hold up our blessings. I do know, that not everyone with wealth and prominence has the right heart or intentions. However, it is not our place to judge that. We only need to put our faith in God. He is All-wise, All-knowing, and All-seeing. It is up to Him to rectify everything according to His will.

The first step to overcoming is to be honest with yourself. Next, identify the roots of the behavior and build your confidence in God. We all want to be successful and looked upon as great men and women. But we must ask ourselves, why do the opinions of others matter so much? I'd been demeaned so much in life that proving my value and worth was everything. I didn't realize that I didn't have anything to prove. I only needed to rest in who God says I am. And to be confident that He would bring every promise to pass in my life. Building my confidence also meant if those around me needed me to hold a particular image laden with luxurious things, they were not the circle I needed. I also worked to maintain an attitude of gratitude. Although I wasn't where I desired to be financially, I was still very blessed. Gratefulness eradicates the idea that more material things equate to more love. Attempting to earn love and affection is idolatry. That is where the pride was for me. My self-image was my idol. I wanted praise, accolades, honor, and attention. I've always thought of myself as humble. However, when ugly behaviors manifest, and God reveals that you need more humility, it is important to submit and surrender. I took the focus off myself and put it on God. I also had to repent for the thoughts in my mind and the envy in my heart. These spirits go far beyond simply desiring what someone else has. They can go into murder if left unchecked. We can look at Cain's example regarding this. Most of you know the story of Cain and Abel, the first sons of Adam and Eve, in Genesis chapter 4. Cain murdered his brother Abel out of jealousy. I'm glad God revealed these things to me so I could repent and uproot the devil's schemes to keep me bound. I renounced those and confessed the word of God over myself.

It took time for me to overcome my frustrations and anger, but the most remarkable part is that God's love for me remained steadfast. It astonishes me that despite my negative and angry thoughts, God saw the finished product beyond my momentary emotional turmoil. If it were anyone else, they might have given up on me, but God loved me despite my shortcomings and continues to do so through every phase of my life. This is why I honor Him with my life. He deserves more than I could ever offer. During times when I contemplated giving up and loathed my circumstances, He intervened and assured me that He had a purpose for my life. Although I could not see it, I trusted and believed in Him because of His unwavering love for me. I am still a work in progress, but I can affirm that my life has dramatically transformed from a person who was angry at God, myself, and my circumstances to someone who wholeheartedly loves God and applies biblical principles to achieve success.

Perhaps you find yourself in a comparable situation, on the verge of giving up due to discontent with your current circumstances. Maybe life has not unfolded as you envisioned, and you are overwhelmed by fear, unhealthy relationships, financial burdens, loneliness, or sin. If this resonates with you,

I want you to know that God loves you exactly where you are. He sent His Son, Jesus Christ, to bear your sins and burdens. God knew that you would stumble repeatedly, yet He saw your inherent worth and desires a relationship with you. Regardless of how chaotic you think your life has become, God has a perfect plan for you. Invite Him into your life and allow Him to make things right. Trust me; He excels at it. You do not have to face your struggles alone. I have been right where you are. I cried out to God for help, and He answered. Believe me, He cares! It is not about denomination, religion, or race. Do not let these factors limit you from becoming the person God created—He sees you as His son/daughter.

Prayer: *God, I need you in every area of my life. There is a lot I do not understand and a lot that I need help with. You are the only one that can fix my situation. I place my life in your hands. Help me surrender it all to you. Give me the peace and strength to overcome my frustrations in Jesus' name. I repent of the sins of envy, jealousy, and coveting. I renounce them in the name of Jesus along with any fruits and roots, including murder, slander, projection, rejection, undermining, contention, discontentment, anxiety, frustration, self-loathing, entitlement, and insecurity. I release and loose brotherly love, contentment, peace of mind, kindness, respect, admiration, celebration, and gratitude, in the Mighty name of Jesus. I repent of idolatry and ask you, Lord Jesus, to create in me a clean heart and renew the right spirit within me. I release and receive pure worship, righteousness, holiness, and humility. I surrender all ill will and ill feelings to you. Help me to be rooted and grounded in your love. Being fully persuaded that You alone are God. You are El-Shaddai, the God who is more than enough. Forgive me for not believing that You are* enough. I receive your grace and mercy in this area and confess that my mind is fortified and resolute. I am a child of the King a joint heir with Christ. You have given me all I need for godliness and life. There is nothing that you will withhold from me as I walk in your statues. Help me to resist getting ahead of your timing. I trust that you know what is best for me and in the proper time, I shall advance according to your word. I put my faith in You. In Jesus Mighty name, Amen.

Take a moment to meditate and reflect. Write down what you feel God is speaking to you through this message.

NAVIGATING LIFE'S FRUSTRATIONS

CHAPTER TWO
I'M NOT FINISHED YET

On my commute to the office, I found myself reflecting on some of the trials I had to endure. It was not a reflection filled with regrets; rather, it was marked by a sense of triumph. The reason behind this victorious sentiment is that my adversaries assumed I would be defeated after subjecting me to their false narratives. Let me tell you, it was a difficult journey. I'd reached a point in life where my personal values and morals seemed meaningless. The path I was on, and the integrity that I tried to live by was overshadowed by the pain. I lost respect for both myself and others, and I could not grasp my own value or my worth. Trust me when I say it was a dark period.

The war against me was set from the moment that I was born. As far back as I can remember, the enemy sought to rob my masculinity, esteem, confidence, and outlook on life. I was tall and skinny in stature, which made me an easy target for bullies in school. The teasing, mockery, and unruly behavior of my peers started the cycle of my negative self-image, and mental anxiety. As I grew into my young adult years, the damaging words replayed over in my mind and robbed my confidence. The enemy knew exactly what he was doing to blind me from my identity in Christ.

Self-rejection is even more damaging than rejection from others. It can cause us to water down our abilities or play it small to avoid rejection. Moreover, it feeds our psyche the fear of never being enough. As I grew into young adulthood, I found the same feelings of low self-worth would surface repeatedly. The feelings of unworthiness had a profound impact on both my business and personal relationships. The wrong word at inopportune times would send me spiraling back into a shell of self-defeat.

Another part of self-rejection is also the inability to receive compliments. I'd often misread and misidentify it as humility. There were several people who saw the greatness masked under my insecurities. I am grateful for those who saw in me what I could not see in myself. Still, their compliments seemed futile. Upon hearing wonderful things spoken to me, I'd often push back, rejecting their affirming words. The reality is that I didn't see in myself what others saw. Because of my lack of confidence, I would devalue my own talents and abilities. While my heart's intent was to show that I didn't consider myself as being above anyone else, it created a false humility. Pride is sneaky and often disguises itself in false humility. Without realizing it, we can dim our own light to appear humble.

An aha! moment for me was the time I applied for a position. Although I was very qualified for it, I wasn't chosen. They told me that I was too humble. Too humble? How is that even possible? Another part of the equation was that I didn't fit into their model. Which means, I'd have to go beyond my moral compass and my ethical character to fit in. I most certainly wasn't going to stoop to any low levels by excluding others and joining in a clique. I've always been the type of person to root for the underdog. I'd choose the most unpopular person or group and make them feel valued and seen. For me, it wasn't an act or a show. I genuinely love people. I know what it is like to feel abated, therefore, it is important to me that each person feels that sense of belonging. However, deep in my soul and spirit was the gnawing sting of rejection. I heard, "too humble" and I internalized it to once again adopt the lie that I wasn't good enough. It took some time for me to recognize the inner healing that needed to be done within my soul. Furthermore, coming to terms that pride also found its way into my fragile self-image. I had to learn to resist the sneaky part of pride that attaches to our emotions and creates hidden defenses. Those defenses can come across as agitations or disingenuous mild mannerisms. It seems an oxymoron to think of pride as both arrogance and inferiority. But it swings on either side, too high of an opinion and too low of an opinion. On the other hand, true humility is defined as the freedom from arrogance and pride and having an accurate estimate of one's worth.[1] To repeat the part (b) of that definition, it says, "having an accurate estimate of one's worth." Due to the offenses, and pain of my childhood, it was difficult for me to have an accurate estimation of my worth. I have no doubt that the interviewers for that position discerned that my lack of self-confidence wouldn't be a right

---

1 https://www.dictionary.com/browse/humility

fit for that position. Ironically, I also knew that I wouldn't fit into their box. And even though I needed to undergo personal transformation, I knew my innate ability to be a leader and not a follower would prove more of a nuisance for them than a blessing. Despite my inner struggles, they did not impede my exceptional work ethic, accomplishments, or the talents I possessed. The great thing about God is when He closes one door, He already has two or more prepared to open.

Because of my lack of confidence, I'd also gone through periods where finding the right connections, friends, and relational partners proved difficult. It seemed that everyone wanted something from me. Thus, their reasons for befriending me were always with ulterior motives. Reflecting on my life, I can see how easily manipulated I was. I spent far too long searching for purpose and relevance without comprehending my own importance. I'm grateful to have broken through those barriers, but unfortunately, it took some time. Because I lacked the realization of how much God loved me, my self-perception could not change.

I consistently stress this fundamental point: when you lack an understanding of your worth, the people around you can exploit your vulnerabilities. They will treat you according to the self-image you hold, which means that when you fail to recognize your value or worth, the likelihood of being taken advantage of significantly increases. Dr. Myles Munroe says it this way, "Whenever purpose is not known, abuse is inevitable."

During those unenlightened years, the trials I faced often left me feeling hopeless, depressed, invaluable, worthless, and empty. I typed more adjectives to describe the darkness that I was in. But in reviewing them, it was too heavy even for me to read. So, I decided to spare you the rest and deleted them. But as you can see, my view of myself was rooted in the lies the enemy planted in my head. Some of which I accepted from people who sought my demise. It is uncanny that we can remain connected to people who want to see us fail. That is another area that must be addressed, because although we long for better acquaintances and connections, we can become addicted to being treated poorly. The devil wants you to fail and will often use those in close association with you to perpetuate his plans.

I learned to take control of my thoughts, because I realized the importance of what I believed about myself carried more weight than the words of my enemies. When you rise in the authority that Jesus Christ died to give you, your life will challenge every false ideology concerning your future. Understanding my position in Christ was crucial to my overcoming defeating thoughts. Ephesians 1:4-5 tells us that God chose us in Him [Christ] before the foundations of the world, that we would be holy and blameless before Him. In love, He predestined us to adoption as sons through Jesus Christ to Himself, according to the kind intention of His will. Paul's words are powerful! Read the entire chapter of Ephesians in your own time. It will be the start of emotional and mental healing as you see your position in Christ, above your present condition. In addition to affirming who you are in Christ, Paul also assures us of the benefits of being chosen by God. You and I have an inheritance. Therefore, know that you are far from finished! It may have taken you more time to achieve your goals, and you may have had to overcome hurdles; however, it does not signify the end. In fact, you are just beginning. Your adversaries failed to grasp that every setback you encountered was only the training ground paving the way for you to fulfill your destiny. While it might appear as though you are not prevailing, the undeniable truth is, that because God stands with you, ready to war on your behalf, victory is guaranteed.

To those who are feeling defeated and broken, I strongly encourage you to shift your mindset. I implore you, at this very moment, to rise and proclaim to your adversaries, critics, and challenging circumstances; "I'm Not Finished Yet!" If you can elevate your mindset above your present struggles, you will gain a glimpse of God's divine outlook, and you will come to realize that things appear significantly brighter from His heavenly vantage point. Changing your mind positions you for victory. When your eyes open to this profound reality, your assurance and faith will ascend to levels that far surpass fear and doubt.

Your journey is far from its conclusion! You are not yet finished; there's still meaningful work ahead of you. It is crucial that you cast aside that (metaphorically speaking) towel you once contemplated surrendering and instead, choose to adjust your vision. Friends, as I continue my journey with renewed determination and a deep understanding of my worth, I want to extend this message to all who may find themselves in the depths of adversity. Remember that life's trials and the doubts planted by others do not define you. For perspectives to change, our understanding must change. Therefore, embrace the power of God and the resilience you have gained by standing strong against the enemy. The challenges you face are shaping you for a purpose greater than you can imagine. So, cast aside any doubts, rise above your circumstances, and with unwavering resolve, declare to yourself and the world, "I'm Not Finished Yet!" Your story is still being written, and the chapters ahead are filled with potential and possibility.

Prayer: *Father, open the eyes of my understanding so that my perspective shifts to my heavenly position in You. On my difficult days, help me to lean into Your love and mercy, so that I may be strengthened by the power of truth. I thank You that my story is still being written and that I am not alone in this battle. I will stand firm on Your promises. When my thoughts overwhelm me, help me to believe and receive your word so that I walk fully into the purpose you predestined before the foundations of the world. In Jesus' name, Amen*

Take a moment to meditate and reflect. Write down what you feel God is speaking to you through this message.

CHAPTER THREE
KEEP FIGHTING

At some point in life, everyone who believes in Jesus Christ will experience attacks from the enemy. It is easy to attribute these attacks to God, but the reality is that since we decided to follow Jesus, hell has been set against us. The good news is that since we have given our lives to the Lord, we now have all of heaven in our corner, fighting with and for us. The Christian Walk consists of different levels, and each level may bring its unique challenges. The closer we are to the next level, the more intense the attacks can become. We hear so much about the blessings that we can forget that trials also exist. I am no stranger to fighting the attacks of the enemy. There was a season when my life took a huge shift. I was in a place where I felt as if my life was going nowhere. I went through a divorce, and at the same time, my dad was battling cancer. I sold cars, so my income was commission-based. As we all know, with divorce comes the responsibility of paying child support. While it can be much at times, I wholeheartedly believe every man and woman is responsible for caring for their children. But with my commission-based income, it was hard to survive and make ends meet. Some days I went without eating because I didn't have funds. I was actively involved in my children's lives, paying child support and dealing with issues on visitation even though I had joint custody. We know that when relationships dissolve, it can lead to unnecessary challenges. Most men are called deadbeats and dragged through the mud even though they do what they should. This mischaracterization can damage an individual's reputation. My peace was more important than anyone's thoughts and opinions of me. I reminded myself of my mother's words, "You are a man now." I had to live up to her words and needed to mature. I had something to prove to myself. So, I did my best to avoid the drama that can come along with leaving a relationship.

The men who have been in this situation understand the pain of court costs, court appearances, and dictated child visitations. We could care less about the money. It's an honor to provide for our children. I speak candidly for most men who share my sentiments on this; it is having to be told or, rather, having a court system design that part of your life. These situations rob us of our voice as fathers. I understand that some men would not provide financially if not forced to do so. But I cannot be silent and fail to give voice to those who earnestly desire to provide. Those who will sacrifice to no end to give the world to their children. Beyond the necessities of life and material needs, there are those of us who desire to steward them well with emotional support, instilling values and affirming them. Life threw me some hard curve balls. Little did I know at the time, it was all a ploy by the enemy to get me into a sunken place of despair and hopelessness. One that would lead me to embark upon self-improvement apart from God.

I was depressed because the amount of child support I had to pay in comparison to the income I brought in did not make sense to me. However, I was subject to the court order. I remember talking to one of my managers at the time, and he tried to encourage me to hustle more so that I would not feel the impact of the financial struggle. As easy as it sounds, my income was at the mercy of people coming in and buying cars. At the same time, my dad was dying of cancer. I didn't know how to respond to life with so many battles going on. It became more unbearable when he passed away. I honestly didn't know how to respond to life.

I wanted to transform my life. I was introduced to a book entitled, *The Secret*. I was referring to this when I stated a few paragraphs up that I tried to rectify my situation apart from God. Here is the funny thing, I employed the steps outlined in this book, and it appeared to be the balm to heal my wounded soul, but it was deception. Its seduction of wealth, prosperity, and peace lured me in. One method for this self-realization was visualization. Each day, one is supposed to set their intentions on their wants and desires by creating a vision board, meditating on desires, and journaling if possible. This was to be done several times a day. *The Secret*, has as its premise the Law of Attraction. The Law of Attraction is said to manifest your experiences through the energy of your thoughts. However, the Bible teaches us that we are to meditate on scripture. Moreover, as believers in Christ, we are warned against idolatry; our focus should be more on God and Jesus Christ than on cars, money, promotion, and relationships. My soul and spirit were at war. I felt the gentle nudges from God beckoning me to put my trust fully in Him. *The Secret* was leading me outside of the parameters of God's will. It is so deceptive that it will essentially replace your identity in Christ with having an identity in material things. It isn't that God does not want us blessed; it's just that God has a timetable, and everything is centered around His glory and your and my purpose in Him. Furthermore, our desires will be manifested as we delight ourselves in Him. I stopped reading *The Secret* and repented before the Lord. Times of vulnerability are often opportunities for the enemy to disrupt God's plans for us. It is dangerous to become so weighed down with life, pain, and struggle that we cannot fully discern God at work amid trials.

I desperately wanted my life to change. That change came with an opportunity to move to Texas. I knew that I needed to jump at the chance to get away from the place that held me in bondage and reset my life. The drawback was leaving my children behind. Up until this point, I'd been able to enjoy our close-knit bond, and leaving them in an entirely different state was unimaginable. Pain gripped my entire being as I thought of not being able to share every moment of watching them grow and develop. Thoughts of being separated from them hurt me to my core. And unfortunately, moving to Texas would work in favor of branding me as a "dead-beat" dad. A term coined for those who do not take care of their children financially, emotionally, or otherwise. It still tugs at my soul because I would never intentionally neglect my responsibility or my parental duties to my children. They are the air that I breathe. But I was about to live out my biggest fear of being away from my children and my rights being dictated by a court? This was the most difficult decision I had to make, but it had to be done.

In relationships, especially marriage, taking responsibility for immaturity, ignorance, and actions is important. Because solidifying the partnership and accountability enables couples to grow and navigate unforseen challenges. Unfortunately, some people marry for circumstances or personal convenience, not realizing these reasons for uniting will take a lot of work and could lead to an unwanted end. In my situation, I was young, immature, and gullible. I didn't know what I was doing but the convictions of my beliefs weighed on me. No one ever intends to contribute to the "single" parenting statistics. Neither do we want our children to be caught between custody battles, child support disputes, or visitation disagreements. When divorce occurs, it affects everyone involved, but men are often blamed and labeled as the reason marriage fails. In these cases, the two adults should learn to co-parent as a whole unit. The decisions should be made together in the best interests of the children. Unfortunately, it doesn't always turn out that way. Keep in mind that this section of the book is not intended to bash or bad mouth my children's mother. We simply were not compatible. As a result, the marriage failed. Additionally, it is my hope that this section ministers to the hearts of men and women who do not understand how the image and identities of men are often skewed by what is portrayed on television, in the news, and in black communities. With this in mind, deliberately painting a negative narrative about the character of a man who is trying their best to be a father and provider can place them in a position to be marginalized and stereotyped by the system that is supposed to foster a greater parental environment and alleviate poverty. When the reverse occurs, it can create distance between the two parents, where the mother doesn't adhere to visitation rights. There is so much more to be said on this subject, but I wanted to convey the emotional distress that came from false accusations during the struggle to keep my head above water. Hearing negative words caused me to question myself and my abilities. I was at a very low point, especially not being able to see my children as much as I wanted to after the move to Texas. Despite my best efforts, my ex and I seemed to be in a constant state of conflict. I didn't know it then, but certain disagreements could have been prevented or resolved had I made better decisions or postponed my responses to the attacks on my character. Our inability to exacerbate our issues was another driving force in my decision to move to Texas.

I was hopeful that moving to Texas would open doors of opportunity for me financially and connect me to people who could help me grow spiritually. It proved to be a huge blessing, but not without the pain of struggle. I couldn't afford airfare to see my children or make court appearances to enforce my granted visitation. I drove over 1000 miles to avoid missing court. I was working on becoming stable so I couldn't afford to pay for airfare for myself and my kids. I had no choice but to take long road trips to visit and pick them up. It was draining emotionally and physically. I was still battling grief and depression from losing my father. Like many, I couldn't see my way out of the horrible situation I was in. I wondered why these things were happening to me. The more I sunk into despair, the more the enemy toyed with my mind. He brought debilitating thoughts of my childhood to mind. My existence seemed framed by the labels put on me by others my entire life. As I thought of all the past pain I'd endured, I found myself searching for answers.

The more I studied God's word, the more I found my why. Remember I kept asking God why I was in those horrible situations? Well, He finally responded..... God ordered my steps before I was formed in my mother's womb. His purpose for my life allowed me to traverse narrow paths. This journey was to lead me back into a full relationship with Him. I'd strayed from God in the natural and my heart. The enemy of our souls presents contradictions in every stage of discovering our identities in Christ. When we are in fellowship with Jesus Christ, we will inevitably face attacks and persecution. It is crucial not to make the mistake of turning these trials into a self-centered narrative. When we focus solely on ourselves, we forget that God said there is more for us than against us.[1] We have myriads of angels at our disposal.

We often experience challenges because of the name we bear and the purpose within us. When we are in the world and doing things apart from God, the enemy would not waste his time afflicting us. His anger blazes against us when we come into the knowledge of who we are in Christ. It is then that we become threats to the kingdom of darkness.

---

[1]   2 Kings 6:16

Yes, there will still be challenges even without salvation, but what joy is there in life without knowing our purpose for living? God desires to reveal that purpose to us, and every day we wake up, an enemy is trying to prevent us from seeking God to discover it. Consider this momentarily: We have the Creator of the universe fighting on our behalf. His objective is for us to understand who He is and the power He has given us. Once we embrace our authority, we understand that we will emerge victorious in every circumstance.

WE ARE NOT ORDINARY

Our value and significance increased the moment we made Jesus our Lord. The old us is gone, and the new us has a place in the Kingdom of God. Knowing that we have a purpose and place in God's kingdom is incredible. I believe that is one of the most uplifting messages we can share with anyone having trouble. If we were merely average, I could understand if we did not embrace or believe in any of the above. But since we are not and know that there is greater inside us, our lives are more than what has happened to us. I know what it is like to feel hopeless. However, because I persisted and pressed through my trials, I know you also have what it takes to press forward. As you've read above, life can sometimes deal some hard blows. I've learned not to be moved by what I see. Therefore, I encourage you to see beyond your now and into the glorious future God has prepared for you.

It's easy to panic when trouble strikes. However, panic will shift you from faith to fear. God did not create us to fear. So, rather than reacting in panic try viewing your situation from God's perspective. It's easier said than done. For me, it required a heart transformation. As I uncovered the roots of my behavior that often led to my poor decisions, I realized that my heart needed healing. I was still carrying the baggage from my past; therefore, my vision was obscured. But once I surrendered fully to God, I also had to make the decision to acquiesce to his leading.

While healing may take time, we must decide to move forward. The best way to navigate this is to seek God first for direction and healing. He has a proven track record. Moreover, He's eager for us to ask, so He can express His love for us and guide us through these situations. Seek Him in prayer and through reading His Word. This alone will boost your confidence to keep fighting. Spending time with God in prayer is one of the most potent tools we must fight with. Allow Him the time to communicate His plan for delivering you from your situation. Remember, our battles are merely training ground for our future.

It is tempting to give up but remember how far you've come. Do not allow circumstances or people to trample over you. Resist the sway of your feelings and emotions. Refuse to let doubt dictate your thoughts about the future. As we continue this journey of faith together, it is important to remember that we indeed have a purpose. Therefore, we must fight through stress, loneliness, anxiety, heartache, and sickness. God is our Healer and Redeemer. He will restore us and make all things new in our lives. Allow me to remind you once again that challenges and battles are an inherent part of our walk with Christ. These trials are not to be seen as punishment or a result of our shortcomings but rather as opportunities for growth and a testament to the purpose we carry. I found strength by embracing my identity in Christ. If you do the same, your purpose will become your driving force.

Prayer: *Father, I need your help through the battles I face. I do not want to be independent but totally dependent on you for everything that concerns my life. Be my strength, hope, and joy through these trials, and help me to overcome in Jesus' name!*

Take a moment to meditate and reflect. Write down what you feel God is speaking to you through this message.

CHAPTER FOUR
EMBRACING LIFE'S THORNS

In life, despite our gifts, anointing, talents, beauty, and blessings, we will encounter our own set of challenges, referred to in the Bible as "thorns." You might be wondering what I mean by "thorns." These are the obstacles that tend to surface just when we are making progress in areas such as life, career, health, or marriage. Digging deeper, in 2 Corinthians 12:7, the Greek word used for thorn in this verse is Strong's 4647 (skol'-ops). It is defined as a sharp affliction; anything producing pain; discomfort; or acute irritation.[2]

From these definitions, we see that a thorn is anything that causes us great discomfort. Thorns can take the form of personal struggles that we're hesitant to share with others, or they may manifest as situations, financial struggles, illnesses, marital problems, etc., that impede us from change, growth, and fulfilling our destiny. However, God's plan for thorns, as narrated through the Apostle Paul, was not to stop or hinder

____

2   https://biblehub.com/greek/4647.htm

his progress; on the contrary, it was to keep him humble as he progressed. What an epiphany! Imagine if we saw those irritants, situations, or even certain individuals whose actions and behaviors are questionable as ordained by God for a specific purpose in our lives.

An intriguing topic, isn't it? When we talk about purpose in the pain, it isn't easily accepted. There are those whose situations are more intense, and at times, the battle may last longer than others, as we long to be free from it, but God doesn't remove the thorn, He instead, allows us to experience the pain that leads us into a deeper revelation of who He is. God is so meticulous that He will allow a thorn not only that we know Him as Father, but Him as the One (The Strength) who dwells on the inside of us.

Each of us face struggles or situations we wish God would remove from our lives. Regardless of the specifics, we all possess something we long to be free from. I understand the frustration and despair that accompany these seemingly unending situations. The easy route would be to give up and accept the situation along with its consequences or attempt to pray the problems away. But that is not always the solution. Have you thought about asking God why you're facing certain situations? I know I might be ruffling a few feathers right now, because most of us have lived under the false notion that we cannot question God. And it sounds deep to ask why not me? Instead of, why me? The truth is we don't want it to be us. If life could be a breeze, we'd all opt for that. Unfortunately, it isn't the easy moments that build our character, faith, and hope in

God. It is those difficult things, and the fiery trials that show us what areas are still under construction. The Bible is replete with scriptures of those who asked God the troubling WHY? During deep pain and anguish our souls long to understand what is difficult to comprehend. The Bible further tells us that we do not have a High Priest who cannot sympathize with us in our hour of weakness. (Hebrews 4:15). That's the assurance! We may not have all the answers, but He will comfort us!

Consider this analogy: a rose is a beautiful flower with an array of colors. Yet, the stem of the rose bears those sharp protrusions called thorns. Notably, the thorn is not at the heart of the rose but is found on its stems. It is the small, painful thing that pricks you when you try to pick up the rose to appreciate its beauty. Although the stem is not entirely covered in thorns, there are still some parts of a rose that have them. Consider this question: Is a rose authentic if it lacks thorns? The purpose of thorns on roses is to discourage herbivores—animals that consume plants—from devouring the leaves that the plant has painstakingly produced. Therefore, thorns serve as a protective mechanism for the rose plant, safeguarding its resources and ensuring its survival. In that analogy, did you catch that thorns can serve as protection?

It is crucial to understand that thorns do not discriminate based on one's color, position in life, or status. Even individuals who outwardly appear flawless have their own share of thorns. The key point here is that these thorns, or challenging situations, as you may choose to describe them, affect everyone indiscriminately. As you've read earlier in this book, I've most certainly had my share of troubles, anxieties, and despairs. But there is another time, that a thorn pierced my flesh so strongly, that it tested my resolve to forgive. I was a member of a particular church. The pastor recognized God's call upon my life and told me he would call on me to preach one of the services. His assignment for me was to prepare at least three sermons and, afterward, allow him to review them. To my surprise, he shared those sermons with other individuals. I heard my words verbatim from another preacher's mouth. I was shocked, angry, hurt, and confused. I felt very betrayed by my shepherd and couldn't believe that he and the other men had the audacity to preach my sermons right in front of me. The revelation that God had given to me was still fresh in my mind, heart, and spirit, so I knew without a doubt he had done something very underhanded. Without damaging the pastor's character, I eventually understood that this test was two-fold. His integrity was being tested, and so was my character. When I finally was given an opportunity to preach, he told me that I only had fifteen minutes. I could feel the heat rise inside of me at the thought. I used every second and preached Jesus Christ. I didn't stop there; I went on to tell the crowd about the words I'd shared with the pastor. Yes, I wanted to be sure that they knew that the sermon he preached was from me. I didn't realize it at the time, but his actions triggered me, reigniting the pain of old wounds. The pain of being betrayed, underestimated, and belittled came rushing back. All those emotions culminated into a greater ball of distrust toward people. I was hurt, once again fractured by the very people that I'd come to admire. This incident was so reminiscent of the pain inflicted on me by countless others in the past. It took a while for divine clarity to reveal that this pivotal moment was a test of wills. I found myself standing at the crossroads, grappling with the choice between letting pride console me by telling the entire congregation the words that he'd spoken were given to him by me, or embrace humility and allow he and his colleagues to claim credit that was undeserved.

Pride/Ego got the best of me in that moment. That thorn was sent to humble me, and I failed that test. Thorns are not always easy to identify. They can be internal as well as external. It takes patience and diligence to see everything through the lens of God. His intentionality amazes me. He is so loving that even when we fail tests, He isn't there to beat us down or judge us. His purpose is always a higher good, an expectant end. This test prepared me for the next one. God didn't rectify the situation. The pastor didn't apologize or admit his wrongdoing. I had a choice, I could either allow bitterness to develop from the betrayal or imitate Jesus and wash the feet of Judas, so to speak. I chose to rise in the All-sufficient grace of God, let the situation go, and forgive them. Humility may not seem like a high road, but as we lean into it, we recognize our own limitations and dependence upon God for validation, security, defense, and progression. He placed within us everything we need for life. Therefore, rather than focus on the pain caused by thorns, we must turn our faces toward God and seek His guidance.

In the second book of Corinthians, Chapter 12, versus 8-10. The Apostle Paul explains that he asked God three times to remove a thorn from his side. However, God's response was,

"No, My grace is sufficient for you." God also told Paul that His strength is made perfect in weakness. Ironically, the Bible doesn't detail what the Apostle Paul's thorn was. Many scholars differ on it, but whatever it was, we know from his own words, that he desperately sought relief from it. He mentioned in the same chapter, that because of the abundance of revelations God had given him, a thorn in his flesh was given to buffet him. Examining the phrase "to buffet" in Greek, gives the impression that it was something very painful.

Although the thorn I mentioned in my own experience may seem light to you, it was crushing for me. There is nothing like God revealing you to yourself. He knew that the spirit of offense was still hiding deep in my soul. I said that I'd forgiven those individuals repeatedly. I'd put in the work to heal and move forward, yet God knew that deep in the crevices of my heart, there was another area where He wanted to apply His grace.

So, you see, the key to success in dealing with life's thorns is to recognize that God's grace is all you need. You must rely on God's strength to carry you through when you are weak. You cannot navigate this life alone. God is right there with you through every challenge and struggle. For me, it was my thorns that made me realize God's grace was enough for everything in front of me. I can genuinely affirm, "If it weren't for my thorns, I would not be here today, sharing the insight: Not all thorns are negative." However, you can overcome them when you depend on God for everything. I share more about fully depending on God in chapter 11.

Listen, the message is clear: thorns are a part of life. Some are allowed, and some are sent directly by God to transform your behavior. Instead of viewing them solely as sources of pain and frustration, consider them opportunities for growth and transformation. Just as the rose would not be as beautiful without its thorns, our lives would not be as meaningful without our challenges. They lead us to seek God, recognize our need for His grace, and build a deeper relationship with Him. They are also beneficial for developing ethical character.

Prayer: *God, thank You for my thorns. I may not fully understand their purpose or benefit, but I ask that You change my perspective so that I may see my situation the way You do. I need You, and I need Your help. Thank You for Your All-sufficient grace, in Jesus' name, Amen.*

Take a moment to meditate and reflect. Write down what you feel God is speaking to you through this message.

CHAPTER FIVE
AWAKEN TO YOUR DIVINE CHOICE

"The person who cannot see the ultimate becomes a slave to the immediate." Dr. Myles Munroe

Life presents us with numerous choices. The paths we choose can either lead us closer to fulfilling our purpose or steer us away from it. I'd eagerly take many do-overs if I had the chance. I'm sure you've also made choices that didn't turn out as expected. This happens when we follow our own paths instead of listening to the voice of God. It may sound like a cliché, but we all have evidence that our decisions have shaped our outcomes. I understand the uncertainty of contemplating the next steps and questioning if we're making the right choices. While we're encouraged to seek guidance and wait for direction, it's important not to wait with anxiety or fear. Fear can immobilize us and prevent us from making any decision, whether right or wrong. Furthermore, living aimlessly devoid of direction will not aid you in walking into your God ordained purpose.

I vividly recall a phase in my life when I grappled with feelings of loneliness and a desperate need for acceptance. These emotions drove me to seek out friendships that I knew deep down held no genuine value for me. Yet, in the throes of loneliness, my vulnerability led to compromise. Consequently, I found myself forsaking my standards and values in a misguided pursuit of acceptance. In doing so, I inadvertently abandoned the identity I discovered in Christ. Though initially appearing enjoyable, the aftermath of misplaced priorities and compromised standards led me down paths I never intended to tread.

I found myself in unfamiliar territory, norms that felt alien to me but were deemed normal by those around me. Although I struggled to function and flourish in those environments, I lingered solely because I'd invested a lot of time into these friendships. I sacrificed a lot and got nothing of value in return. It was a disheartening experience, to say the least. While my intentions were pure, without fully realizing it, I squandered valuable time and didn't reap any personal benefits. This realization eventually prompted me toward repentance.

In retrospect, it appeared to be a central pattern. I stayed in relationships and friendships longer than I should have. I've kept quiet when I should have spoken up and I've invested time and energy into things that proved unprofitable for me. I'm not ashamed to admit that in my human frailty, I did what I thought would benefit me, but it only benefited others. It takes great fortitude to walk away from toxic relationships or simply those that are one-sided, lack integrity, and are devoid of growth.

We've heard it said, "People are in our lives for a reason and a season." It is important not to hold on to things, people, jobs, etc., when the season has shifted. Luke 14:28 tells us that no one desires to build a tower without first calculating the cost. (NLT-Paraphrased) Understand that the "cost" includes more than monetary pricing. It involves taking a realistic assessment, thoughtful consideration, weighing the consequences, and carefully strategizing. Counting the costs also means knowing when to cut your losses. Yes, there are times when we must make tough decisions. You've already read about my decision to relocate and how difficult it was to pack up and leave everything that I knew behind me. We must consider the long-term values, risks involved, and if it is a short-term investment, we must accurately ask ourselves what benefits do we hope to gain. Of course, the list isn't exhaustive. Depending on the decision, the research will undoubtedly change, but this is just to let you know that as we grow older, the wiser we should become in choosing things that add to our lives rather than subtract the value that God has placed on the inside of us. Do you sense God shifting you in a different direction? What is He speaking to you? Do you feel yourself at a crossroads in life? If so, keep reading.

When you recognize your worth and prioritize your well-being, you'll come to cherish your identity and discover that your life is meant to fulfill a higher purpose. Truthfully, in most cases, we and I use the word "we" loosely because it may not be your testimony. However, we tend to make decisions based on what is presented before us without doing any due diligence. When we choose based on what we feel or what we perceive about something, chances are we can end up taking the wrong route. My past decisions have landed me in some tough spaces. At certain moments, I pondered whether I would ever break free from the entanglements and chaos.

Let's delve briefly into a biblical narrative. Genesis 12:1 tells us that God told Abram to leave his country, and not only his country but his father's house and travel to the place that He would reveal to him. In the following verses of that same chapter, God outlines the blessings He had in store for Abram if he would follow His instructions. God didn't give Abram the exact location of his next move, which shows us that God doesn't always give complete instructions. In obscurity, He invites us to trust that He knows best, and He will always fulfill His Word towards us. We also see that although Abram was given a direct command, he still had the choice to fully obey God and leave the place of familiarity, and move forward into inheriting his promises. Verse 5 of that same chapter reveals that Abram left the city of his birth as God commanded. If we dig deeper into the narrative, we will discover that Abram's journey had its challenges. God required that he leave his old life completely, and His requirements for us today remain the same. To inherit the promises He has for us, we will likewise have to leave former habits, lifestyles, and some individuals behind. I find it interesting that Abram was in his seventies, and God still called him to do great things. A friend of mine was sharing with me a teaching he did on the life of Abraham. And just in case you are not aware, God changed Abram's name to Abraham in connection with the covenant He made with him; the covenant that He continues to maintain with us (His people) today. The name change occurred in Genesis chapter 17. I wanted to share that because I cannot assume that everyone who reads this book is familiar with the Bible or that narrative. Therefore, you will notice the interchange of names Abram and Abraham written here.

As my friend and I continued our conversation, he shared the richness of the word he was studying on Abraham who is also referred to as, "The Father of the Faith." He followed God completely, and that title was bestowed upon him. Imagine having so great a faith that your name goes down in the hall of fame. Not because you hit the Forbes list or anything of great prestige; but because your faith in God prompted such a great an obedient heart that it set the standard for future generations. It moved me because the Bible is so immeasurable. Passages can be passed over without us grasping the full revelation. Intriguingly, my friend did mention Abraham's great wealth. He pointed out that even though he had wealth, he didn't build lavish buildings or housing, but the Bible says that he pitched a tent. As I meditated on the word of God, I received further revelation. Pitching tents was synonymous with showing that he was a sojourner in the land. In obedience to God, he knew that the places he traveled would not to be his permanent dwelling place. He also built altars to worship God. His life was characterized by his obedience and worship. Look at Hebrews 11: 8-10, "By faith, Abraham, when he was called, obeyed, by going out to a place which he was to receive for an inheritance; and he left, not knowing where he was going. By faith, he lived as a stranger in the land of promise as in a foreign land, living in tents with Isaac and Jacob, fellow heirs of the same promise, for he was looking for the city which has foundations, whose architect and builder is God." (NASB)

Concerning this revelation and what it means for us today, I heard God say too many people are comfortable living in places that no longer have the capacity to house what they hold. The name Abram is related to his old identity, which meant exalted father. The (new) name Abraham means "father of a multitude." God is purposeful in everything that He does. The name change signified the fulfillment of God's promises. I am still processing this word as I move into the new territory God has given me. We know it took Abraham's faith to move from his kindred's land to the place God would later reveal. He had a divine choice to make. We often fear the unknown. As a result, many of us do not move because we do not have the entire blueprint. But God is calling us to trust Him. The flipside of moving forward is doing so with the same mindset and not allowing faith to flourish. Don't confuse contentment with being comfortable. Take the Apostle Paul; He said, "I learned to be content in whatsoever state I am in" (Philippians 4:11-13). Paul didn't say comfortable. Comfort keeps you in environments where you feel you can control everything. This is a problem because if you stay in a situation out of comfort, you are choosing to stay stagnant. Seasons of life involve growth. As you grow, you are stretched. The stretching will be uncomfortable if you have outgrown the current place.

AWAKEN TO PURPOSE

We've often squandered precious time on pursuits that leave us questioning the purpose of life, while all along, God has been declaring, "I am right here, and I have a purpose for you" (Jeremiah 29:11-13). His plan far surpasses anything we could envision for ourselves. Meriam Webster defines purpose as something set up as an object or end to be attained: intention, resolution, determination.[1] The verbal root of the Hebrew word for purpose means to give counsel, deliberate, or to determine. Ecclesiastes 3:1 says, "To everything there is a season, a time for every purpose under heaven." (NKJV) God has not only given us purpose, but according to this Scripture, whatever you were born to do, God has assigned a season in which it is to be done and completed.

In the New Testament, a key passage of scripture is found in Ephesians chapter 1:9-11. Apostle Paul explains that God brings all things under Christ in conformity with the purpose of His will. The whole economy of God is linked with His purpose.[2] It is imperative to understand that our primary purpose is to please God. We do this by our obedience to His word. Next, by using the talents and gifts He has given us to advance His Kingdom and impact the world around us. Ecclesiastes 3:10 says, I have seen the burden God has laid on men. The word burden is used in different Bible translations as a *heavy responsibility, a load, occupation, task, or a responsible urge.* Vines Expository dictionary defines it as *something to be borne.*[3] With these definitions in mind, what is weighing on your heart and spirit? What burden or responsibility do feel called to fulfill?

---

1. https://www.merriam-webster.com/dictionary/purpose
2. https://www.biblestudytools.com/dictionary/purpose. Copyright © 1996 by Walter A. Elwell. Published by Baker Books, a division of Baker Book House Company, PO Box 6287, Grand Rapids, Michigan 49516-6287
3. Vine's Complete Expository Dictionary of Old and New Testament Words. T. Nelson, 1984/Burden.pg.83

Understanding purpose is essential to enjoying the life God has given us. Doing everything with vision and purpose in view will keep us from being pulled into activities and ventures that do not emanate from God's purpose for us. Dr. Myles Munroe said, "The most frustrated person is the one without vision and purpose." Psalm 33:11 says, "The plans of the Lord stand firm forever, the purposes of his heart through all generations." You may be wondering what discovering purpose has to do with making great choices and decisions. The answer is everything! The choices and decisions you make in life will determine how much you do with what you have.

I find that it is difficult to focus on pleasing God when our lives are consumed with challenges. Often, the challenges of life will cloud our focus, and demand our time and mental energy. During these times it is crucial to break free from feelings of victimhood and self-pity to take meaningful steps forward. Do not expend your energy in self-doubt because it will create a greater level of stagnation. To progress and move forward, it is vital to recognize that real life happens. And as it does, we must mature in our expectations and our faith. Faith in action doesn't necessitate a do-nothing mentality. Life isn't to be gambled away. On the contrary, living by faith is believing what God says about you and the power you possess. In addition to believing, you must also employ pragmatic steps to secure success. Simply put, "faith without works is dead."[4]

As you self-reflect, it is vital that you do not beat yourself up over past mistakes and poor choices. Most of us learn by

---

4. James 2:17

doing. However, if you find repeated patterns/cycles of the same mistakes in your finances, relationships, jobs, with your spouse, children, etc. it is a sign that you need to re-evaluate your thinking and decision making. Just like the Israelites, God will let you go around the same mountain, until you decide to choose obedience!

I can relate to feelings of stagnation, and wondering what I had done that was so wrong to land me in the places of such pain and uncertainty. I've always been a forward thinker, and able to excel above my peers, however, I'd come to a place where everything around me seemed to be crashing down, and I felt powerless and empty. I fought with every ounce of strength to keep my head above water. When I grew sick and tired of being sick and tired, my heart desired more than what I was currently living. I knew that there was more for me, but I had to choose. Either I'd break the pattern of shrinking in my gifts and talents to be accepted or remain in that same stale, stagnant place that would not allow me or my seed to soar. I decided it was time to let go of the things that were not serving my purpose and focus on fulfilling God's mandate for my life. My surroundings had to change. Before, I was held captive by my need to be validated and accepted. I chose to hang around people who didn't have the same mindset that I had. In essence, I settled for friendships that were safe. They were friendships that didn't challenge me nor drive me toward achieving my goals. It was just a circle that served my ego. The time that I spent hanging out with this group was time that led me away from my pursuit of God. Therefore, I chose to put myself in a place with people who were visionaries. Those who chose to live integral and treat me with the respect that I deserved. It dawned on me that while it took considerable time to establish myself in life, it took just a fleeting moment to veer off course. Despite my identity being rooted in Christ, the allure of acceptance had become my primary focus. I had to confront the reality that I'm not called to pursue every friendship or relationship. The calling I've received from God doesn't grant me a grace card to partake in every social circle or connection. The acceptance of others should not dictate or alter the path God has set before me or you.

Like me, you have a choice, you can opt to remain where you are, or you can choose to go before God, seek His guidance to achieve everything He has in store for your life. Just because your current circumstances have been your norm until now does not mean they can't or won't improve. There are always alternatives, even in the most challenging situations. Please understand that quick and painless solutions are not always the best answers. Because they offer little to no encouragement towards growth, maturity, and or gratitude. It is often our reluctance to face challenges and make necessary changes that leads us to passively endure whatever life throws at us. It is fear that typically drives this mindset and leaves us feeling mentally paralyzed and trapped. This preconditioning causes us to believe that there are crowns without crosses. However, this mindset is antithetical to the Bible. God never promised us that life would be void of pain. But God also reassures us that despite the pain, we still have a choice. We can allow it to govern the decisions that we make or we can choose to break away from the societal conditioning that has shaped our thinking. When we turn to God, and gain His perspective we will experience Him work everything out in our favor.

Going back to Abram's narrative in Genesis chapter 12, one would think at Abram's age that he would have already reached his destiny. Perhaps you share those same feelings. Maybe you feel as if you have reached a plateau, a place where age is catching up to you, or because of your poor choices, you will never reach your ultimate place of destiny. But regardless of the circumstances you find yourself in, or wrong decisions you have made, Jesus has made the ultimate sacrifice to provide you with an opportunity for a different path. The choice to welcome Him into your life is entirely yours; He will not impose Himself upon you. You might say, "I've tried that before, and it did not work." I understand those sentiments because I have walked that same road and shared those same doubts. However, when I reached a point of utter dissatisfaction with the relentless cycle of life, I consciously decided to surrender completely to God and allow Jesus to take the wheel. Now, I can genuinely attest to a remarkable transformation. My mind has undergone a profound renewal that has altered my thinking. My relationships have blossomed, and my finances have seen positive shifts. I am no longer enslaved by sin, defeat, depression, anxiety, or guilt. Everything in my life shifted in Christ. I am a new creation; the old has passed away, and all things have become new (2 Corinthians 5:17). This joy that greets me each morning - freedom in Christ Jesus!

Do not get me wrong, I am not saying that I do not have challenges, but I am stating that because of Jesus Christ, I handle them differently. With that being said, I believe that we all have a choice. We can choose to change and become all that we were created to be, or we can ignore what God is saying to us right now and stay trapped where we are. You have options, but the choice is completely up to you. Do not make the mistake and dismiss this message as if it does not apply to you. All of us have fallen short, and some have backslidden, but God still patiently waits for us to surrender to His divine will. At some point in life, we will all have to reposition ourselves to have a greater impact, and be productive in every area of our lives. Nothing stays the same. We see technology, church, how we conduct business, and education consistently shift; therefore, we must evolve with life. That evolution cannot occur without wholeness in Christ. When we take another look at Abram, we find although he obeyed God to leave his father's house, he took his father and his nephew Lot, along with him. Eventually, the place where they dwelled became a place of great conflict. That conflict led to a separation between him and his nephew. Abram was still tied to his past. Unless we experience a mental transformation, we will be tempted to drag the old into the new life that Jesus Christ died to give us. Apostle Paul tells us to be renewed by the transforming of our minds. (Romans 12:2).

As I conclude this message, I want you to understand the deep resonance of hope and transformation within these words. My heartfelt sentiment is for each of you to break free from any sense of helplessness or self-pity that may be holding you back. The thought-provoking questions I have presented below are meant to guide you towards self-discovery and spiritual growth. They are to help you grasp the profound importance of your relationship with God. Always remember that God's love for you knows no bounds, and His sacrificial act opens the door to positive change and a life transformed by faith.

1. What do you sense God is conveying to you in this present moment?

2. Is there a specific aspect of your life that He is encouraging you to release or let go of?

3. Are there any profound insights or lessons that He is aspiring to reveal to you in this moment?

4. Considering your spiritual journey, where is your current focus directed?

5. Do you believe in the potential for transformative change in your life?

6. Finally, in response to his divine guidance, what actions do you intend to take?

7. What holds the greatest importance for you at this moment?

8. Are you weary of the repetitive patterns?

9. Where are you in your relationship to God, Jesus Christ and the Holy Spirit?

10. Do you long for a deeper relationship with God?

These questions may seem overwhelming, but their answers are key to evaluating your life. With all that I have shared in this book thus far, the enemy may still plague you with doubts about God and your abilities to achieve the life that you desire. But allow me to assure you that such doubts are unfounded. Believing that God is indifferent or distant from you is false. In truth, God's love for you is immeasurable, evidenced by His willingness to sacrifice His own Son for your sake. This sacrifice provides the opportunity to bring about positive changes and improvements.

This is your defining moment, a golden opportunity for a fresh start. God is acutely aware of your current position in this chapter of your life. Despite any past misconceptions or beliefs, it is crucial to recognize that He desires nothing less than the very best for you. Again, this does not promise a life devoid of challenges, but it does assure you that when you encounter difficulties, His unwavering presence stands ready to guide you through them.

In the end, the power of choice rests firmly in your hands. You can choose to embrace change, step into the person you were destined to become, or remain ensnared by your present circumstances. God patiently awaits your decision. So, I ask you: What will you do? Your brightest days are still ahead of you, and the path to a fulfilling life awaits your choosing to move ahead in boldness.

Prayer: *God, thank you for the opportunity you give us to choose. I have made many mistakes and I confess them all to you. I sincerely ask you to forgive me, cleanse me, and make me a new creation in you. I surrender my life to you, and I submit to your will. Have your way in my life, in Jesus' name! Amen*

Take a moment to meditate and reflect. Write down what you feel God is speaking to you through this message.

54

CHAPTER SIX
IN THE WAIT

God tells us to be anxious for nothing. Yet most people fall into the trap of impatience, which is often fueled by comparisons. It is difficult to look at others acquiring the things that we desire at a faster rate than we acquire them. In doing so, we can often wonder what is wrong in our lives and or allow the enemy to plant lies telling us that we need to do more ourselves to acquire them. If we are not careful, fear will grip us and cause us to become reactive in making hasty decisions. It has become increasingly apparent that we are all on an unwavering quest to reach predefined destinations and accomplish our goals. What's disheartening is that this perpetual rush has deeply ingrained itself into our nature. It is as if we are sprinting through life.

We often fail to acknowledge the profound advantages of patience, overlooking the transformative power it can have on our journey. Patience holds significant importance because, during moments of waiting, God isn't idle; rather, He is working to develop the capacity and character within you to handle what He has for you. Therefore, it is vital that you realize there is a sequence to everything. The Bible refers to it as a "time" for everything. For example, when you enter a restaurant, you are greeted by the host, seated, then a server approaches your table, introduces him/herself, and, proceeds to take your drink orders, and explains any specials for the day and ask if you'd like to order any appetizers. After bringing your drinks to the table the server asks if you are ready to order your meal. Each step serves a purpose. Enjoying your drink orders will give you time to peruse the menu, while appetizers keep your hunger at bay until your meal arrives.

This meticulous process is designed to minimize complaints and rushing. Now, consider your goals and dreams. What if you reach them too soon? What if they materialize before you are adequately prepared? You might be frustrated, not realizing that if you had waited for God's timing, you would have arrived precisely when you were meant to. Even though the journey may be lengthy, you will receive everything He has in store for you at the perfect moment.

I can admit that waiting can be a challenge. I certainly understand the struggle of waiting; I have been there. I have made hasty decisions and attempted to expedite God's plan for me. Trust me when I say this: I could have spared myself a great deal of stress and frustration if I had waited. I remember when I was living in my apartment after my second divorce. I told God that I was never getting married again because it wasn't worth it. If I am being honest, I made the decision to marry previously without wisdom and for convenience. In my immaturity, I made those commitments knowing I did not have the capacity to fulfill them.

I take accountability for my actions and the people I have hurt along the way. I own them! And I apologize. Everyone should desire good and healthy relationships, but the partners we choose should also be the ones God has predestined us to be joined with. Maybe yours isn't the story of impatiently waiting for marriage. Maybe it's a position, promotion, or financial breakthrough, but regardless of what it is you are waiting for, you must ask yourself, why am I in such a hurry? Are you trying to shut down haters and prove your value to them? Do you believe time is running out? Has age made you think time is running out? As you ponder the answers to these questions, I want you to know the good news is if you are in Christ Jesus, time is on your side. Age has no bearing on His usage of you. Since you are His creation, He knows precisely when you will be ready and mature enough for what He's been preparing for you. Yes, waiting can be stressful and occasionally disheartening, but what awaits you is well worth the patience. You might be thinking, "I do not have the strength to wait." But I have a scripture to counteract that sentiment: Isaiah 40:31, "But they that wait upon the Lord shall renew their strength; they shall mount up with wings as eagles; they shall run, and not be weary; and they shall walk, and not faint." (KJV) According to this scripture, you will end up running without growing weary, walking without fainting, and soaring higher than your current position. Eventually your weariness will transform into joy. There is something greater ahead, but you must wait for it. Do not rush. Do not hasten your journey. Keep your heart focused on the Lord. Wait on Him, and He will fortify your heart.

There was a time impatience gripped my soul. After my divorce, I struggled financially, but I was ok with it because my peace was priceless and not up for compromise. I remember days going without food. When my coworkers asked me out to lunch, I'd have to decline if they were going somewhere other than Taco Bell or McDonald's. The dollar menus at those places satisfied me without me having to convey my struggles or ask for help. I was silent about my financial burdens because I hated the thought of anyone knowing. It made me feel like less of a man. While I know that was not the truth, those were the thoughts I wrestled with then. Eventually, some of my co-workers noticed that I only ate at Taco Bell and McDonald's and embraced me regardless of the amount of money I had. Their kindness gave me the courage to be transparent, because I knew I could trust them. They were angels in disguise.

When I moved to Texas, I met Pastor Leo, who mentored and treated me like I was his son. He and his wife, Pastor Linda, prayed for me and ensured that I had food when I got custody of my son. I had been serving as the sound man in church with no intention of getting paid for it. I was faithful to go and serve, although putting gas in the car was also a struggle, and I was ordered to pay back child support, although I currently had custody of my son. However, Pastor Leo always gave me something to help me get by until my situation changed. God knew exactly what I needed and provided it. I wasn't accustomed to experiencing God's love through people, but these acts helped me to trust God more.

I began to get prophetic words about the ministry God was calling me to fulfill. I was familiar with the prophetic, but this felt very different. Some of the prophetic words I got were about financial breakthroughs and the marketplace anointing. In my mind, I was thinking, "Okay Lord! I don't understand, but okay." I was ready for something different and wanted to walk in what God called me to do. I was hesitant but anxious. Remember a few chapters back I mentioned the time I prepared sermons, and they were given to other ministers to preach? Because of that, I was still battling with trust. It seemed like everything weighed me down. I also remember receiving a prophetic word about the wife God had for me. The prophet said that she would love me beyond my current circumstances. Even after receiving that word, I was in a very callous place mentally. I went through all kinds of mind battles. And I told God that I was done, and I would not get married again. I was embarrassed enough that I went through two divorces and had a lot of child support to pay. Having gone through two divorces, and the stigma around child support, caused me to wrestle with shame and embarrassment. I felt like anyone who knew my situation would judge me. And even though I was adamant that marriage was off the table, a part of me still longed for love and a happy marriage. Truthfully, I was afraid that no one would see the real me and still desire to love me. As much as I battled, the prophecies kept coming. Another time, I received a prophetic word that the wife God had for me was also praying for me. I didn't respond when I received that word. Instead, I held back how I felt until I got home. I said to God,

"You play too much!" Who am I to say that to the Father? But honestly, that's how I felt. My thoughts were centered around the negativity about my divorces and the criticism that came from them. I needed God to deliver me from people's opinions because the ridicule and judgment fed my insecurities.

It seemed as if people everywhere picked up on my desire for a wife; and someone was prophesying to me about a wife. The next word I received was, *"The wife God has for you will be drawn to you, and you will be drawn to her."* At that point, I started to pay attention to these prophecies. Either they all picked up on my inner desires, or God really had marriage designed for my destiny. Each word came from different people, including strangers, so I started to look at them as confirmations.

However, as time passed and marriage didn't appear to be in sight, I came to a point where I got tired of waiting. So, I started searching again. I was dating with the expectation to find the wife God had for me. I remember dating a woman who I thought had potential, but God said otherwise. The clutch in my truck went out and I had to have it replaced. My friends Jay and Jennifer, who are family to me, followed me to drop off my truck. Shortly after getting into the car with them, Jennifer told me that God had just given her a word for me. She was a little hesitant to say it, but Jay encouraged her to go ahead and release it. The word was, "God said the wife he has for you will blow your mind, but the one you are dating," and I quote, "Ain't it." I could understand her hesitancy. Some people are offended at words from God, because they think He only gives positive words to His prophets. I beg to differ! I received the word she gave and immediately had a conversation with the woman I was dating.

When we are impatient and want things to happen on our timetable, we can end up in relationships or situations that are not a part of God's plan for our lives. We cannot rush God, or force things to happen in our time. What would have happened if I was not obedient to the word God gave me? I could have ended up with another broken relationship. And, If I pushed ahead into ministry, I could have delayed what God wanted me to do. Waiting, though difficult, is not a bad thing. Perhaps you haven't received a prophetic word concerning your future, you do have the Bible. Within its pages, God reminds us that His plans are to prosper us and to give us a future and a hope. (Jeremiah 29:11). I've shared how much I struggled in various seasons. I've dealt with trauma, loss, lack, and ridicule. I know what it feels like to feel as if God isn't coming through fast enough, and to have negative voices cause you to question your own life and faith. I also know how to look and sound like everything is normal and okay, while fighting with every ounce of strength just to maintain your sanity. These are the times when waiting can seem more like a burden than a blessing. It can even appear as if God is not listening and will not answer your prayers. It is imperative that you do not give in to those feelings; instead trust that God is working everything out for your good. Our hope comes out of the confidence of knowing who God is. The more we know Him, the greater our confidence will be that He is capable of doing exactly what He says.

Keep pressing toward your goals and believing every

dream will come to fruition. Remembering that it is in those fiery trials that God pulls out the best in us. As we cling to Him, and press into hope, we will avoid sinking deep into despair, desperation, and coveting. There is danger in making decisions out of desperation. Out of desperation, we can fall into the devil's traps of lying, manipulation, scheming, and even thievery. We may very well forfeit the great blessings that God has prepared for us, because He takes the way that we wait very seriously. He warns us against being anxious because He knows what anxiety can do to the body and the mind. He knows that it opens the door for greater spirits of fear and control. Therefore, rather than allowing false perceptions of what someone else has or how their lives may contrast with yours keep your focus on God. Look back over your life and remember what God has already done. You will see like a carefully orchestrated puzzle; the pieces seem to fit. No matter where you are on this journey, nothing gets wasted when used to propel you further and deeper into God's plan. His past faithfulness will help you look forward to the future with hope and great expectation. Do not listen to the voices of others as they attempt to talk you out of your vision. Romans 4:20 tells us that Abraham never wavered concerning the promise of God. But he grew stronger in his faith and continued to give God glory as he was fully convinced that God was able to do exactly as He promised.

I love that God understands every emotion that we will experience in this human frame. The Bible tells us that we do not have a High Priest who cannot sympathize with us in our weakness, for He was tempted in every way that we are, yet did not sin. (Hebrews 4:15). Here, we are reminded that God's grace covers us and infuses us with the power to overcome our anxious thoughts, and moments of self-doubt. He gives us the beautiful example of our Lord and Savior, who remained steadfast without sin. I know when we mention sin, we think of big sins, but worry, doubt, and anything that does not come from faith is sin. James 1:12, tells us that God blesses those who patiently endure testing and temptation. Afterward, they will receive the crown of life God has promised to those who love Him.

There are layers of patience. God allows us to develop it through circumstances and with difficult people. The more the fruit of patience manifest in us, the more we discover, areas where unhealed emotions got us outside of the will of God. Then, we are then matured to bear up under difficult circumstances. That is exactly what patience is: the capacity to accept or tolerate delay, trouble, or suffering without getting angry or upset.[1] Moreover, it gives us supernatural restraint and enables us to behave more loving, kind, and gentle towards others. Patience is also the supernatural outcome of walking in the Spirit, not the flesh. It allows time for God to prepare you for what He has for you and time for God to heal you from your past mistakes and heartbreak. It also allows God to mature you into your promise. I now have the wife God designed for me. She was worth the wait! At the time I met her, I didn't realize she was my wife, but previously, I'd asked God to reveal her to me. We had a mutual friend, and I thought that she was beautiful. But <u>my fear and focus</u> was on my insecurities and circumstances.

1.Https://www.oxfordlearnersdictionaries.com/us/definition/english/patience.

Remember the Word I received? *"She isn't going to care about any of that, and she's praying for you."* Well, it was true; on our first date she and I talked for hours, and she confirmed that I possessed all the qualities she desired and prayed for in her mate. We've been inseparable ever since. This has been a beautiful prophetic journey of love and commitment with Christ at the center. I'm grateful that I was obedient to what God revealed and didn't forfeit through desperation.

In the past, impatience has caused me a lot of mistakes. It has also caused me some delay and frustration; nevertheless, God continues to love me and has not altered His course for my destiny. Another component of patience is found in 1 Thessalonians 1:3, "As we pray to our God and Father about you, we think of your faithful work, your loving deeds, and the <u>enduring hope</u> you have because of our Lord Jesus Christ." With this in mind, do your utmost to persevere through whatever lies before you. Stand firmly upon His word and understand that some things are genuinely worth the wait. Only God can define what your waiting season is all about. Seek His face and allow Him to guide you. He will reveal whether you are being prepared, protected, or being taught a lesson in obedience through discipline. Remember, the Israelites wandered in the wilderness for forty years because of their disobedience. (Joshua 5:6). Keep trusting God and know, without a shadow of a doubt, that patience is having its perfect work in you.

Prayer: *Father, I know that I am impatient and rushing to reach my goals. Please forgive me and give me the grace I need to wait with patience. Help me to have joy on this journey and peace* *where I need it most. Forgive me for comparing my life with others. Help me to walk in gratitude for each step that I am on. I come before You today with a heart full of trust and hope, seeking Your divine guidance and comfort. Lord, I acknowledge that Your plans for me are perfect, and Your wisdom surpasses all understanding. Yet, in my human frailty, I sometimes struggle with impatience and doubt, please forgive me. Father, help me to focus on You and enlarge my capacity to see the bigger plan for my life. As I take these moments of waiting to grow and learn, help me to wait upon Your timing. Help me to trust that each moment of waiting is part of Your greater plan and purpose for my life. Fill my heart with Your peace that surpasses all understanding, and allow me to rest in the assurance that You are in control. Teach me, Lord, to rely entirely on Your guidance. When I feel anxious, afraid, or uncertain, remind me of Your promises and the countless times You have been faithful. Because You have been so faithful! Strengthen my faith so that I may remain steadfast, even when the path ahead is unclear. I know as I put my hope in You, my hope will never fail. Thank You, Father, for Your infinite love, grace, and mercy. Help me to grow in patience and trust, knowing that Your plans for me are good and filled with hope for the future. I surrender my worries and desires into Your capable hands, believing that Your timing is perfect. In Jesus name, Amen.*

Take a moment to meditate and reflect. Write down what you feel God is speaking to you through this message.

CHAPTER SEVEN
CHOOSE YOUR BATTLES

I'm not a confrontational person. However, there are social media posts, podcasts, or conversations will rub me the wrong way and I want to defend or correct the person posting and or speaking. But I try to remember, not everything is my battle. There are also times when my compassionate heart will want to jump in and help everyone, but I know it isn't wise to take on every burden. It is crucial that we discern when the enemy wants to distract us from our purpose through others and our emotions. I have a saying that I try to employ in my everyday life. "If it doesn't affect my destiny, I'm not interested in it."

Conflicts are a part of life, whether they happen in professional settings, personal relationships, family, and or in societal environments. No two people will agree all the time. However, how you choose to deal with conflict or walk away from it will prove your level of growth, maturity, and ability to handle interpersonal relationships with sound judgment. Not every conflict is worth addressing. Many disagreements are trivial and are not worth it in the long run. When you ask yourself if what's bothering you now will matter one year from now, chances are it won't, and it's better to focus on the things that have a bearing on your future. Every battle has a cost. These costs include time and the emotional drain of engaging in the conflict. Even if you win the battle, maybe your time and energy could have been better spent elsewhere. Victory isn't all that matters, sometimes, there are other factors to think about, as we all have limited time on earth. You and I will die someday. When you look back over your life from your deathbed, what do you want to see? A life where you argued with everyone who stood in your way, or a meaningful life well lived? The point of choosing your battles is to be protective of how you spend your time, which is a limited resource. What are the things that are important to you? What are your most important goals? Who are the most important people in your life? When you waste valuable time and energy, eventually, you will exhaust yourself. But by carefully choosing your battles, you reserve your time for the important things and win the bigger wars.

I mentioned the turmoil in some of my relationships in previous chapters. It took a lot of growth and unlearning to evolve from conflicts and disagreements that had no significance. During my immaturity, winning an argument was everything. I'd always been the person to try to find a resolution, but when pushed to my limits or if I felt I wasn't being heard, I'd shut down. However, there is a constructive and intentional approach to resolving issues. When things are done maturely, it fosters deeper trust and mutual understanding. Without the end-goal to collaboratively find an amicable resolution, disagreements turn into one-sided and unproductive wars.

I vividly recall an incident where I applied for a new position at a company where I was employed. I was interviewed by several leaders in a panel-style interview. Afterward, an acquaintance who was also on the panel told me that there was some negative conversation regarding me and the position that I was interviewing for. She mentioned that it was said that I was too "religious" and was adamant about my beliefs around the office. I knew that the words spoken about me were not true because, although I love God and am an advocate of Jesus Christ, I never force my faith on anyone.

Everything within me wanted to address what was said about me in that "private" discussion. However, I had to choose to keep my acquaintances' confidence. It took diligent resolve to let it go and leave it in the hands of God. It is human nature to want to defend ourselves. However, we must always leave room for God to fulfill His word as our Defender. Admittedly, it can be tough to hear negative words and comments spoken about us that are untrue, but taking the high road always yields a greater reward.

If I had allowed my intellect to be overruled by emotions, I could have caused greater conflict within the office, and hindered my ability to be promoted. Flesh always wants to react, but I chose to bring my thoughts and emotions under subjection to the character of Christ. As a result, God gave me a promotion in another department. I could have forfeited that promotion, battling over something that wasn't mine in the first place. Again, if it doesn't affect my destiny, it doesn't get my attention.

We must also think before we speak and react. What if the information my acquaintance told me concerning my character was misconstrued or misstated? What if it was said to incite division or mess? Thankfully, I knew that she wasn't that type of person, but there are people who do not operate in integrity. There are those who purposely sabotage relationships, and other people's advancement opportunities. In either case, it is better to let God deal with individuals than behave immaturely.

Mastering the art of choosing wisely may be a lot to undertake, however, it will save the relationships that align with your core values, and destiny. Remember it is impossible to evade all conflict, and some conflicts are necessary to show you what is inside of you. Some people don't realize that they can be triggered until they are. Some don't realize that rejection still looms in their souls, until they face it. Therefore, all conflict isn't bad. Consider this: some conflict is designed by God to mature you in your emotions. Choosing peace over self-protection in arguments and disputes will stretch your capacity to lead in different areas of life. There is always someone somewhere who is watching your behavior and awaiting your response. This isn't to say to put on false airs of who you are; it is to remember that everything you do has a ripple effect, and someone else will be affected by how you choose to fight your battles.

AVOIDING TRAPS

Have you ever been pulled into someone else's battle or conflict? At times entertaining conversations or being the ear and shoulder for someone else will expose you to a battle that is not intended for you. But because of your relationship with the person their offense, problem, or issue will become yours. This can be a matter of defending them, and or taking on the weight of their problem. Before long, you can find yourself being angry or responding to the person they also have conflict with, either verbally or in your heart. There are also times, through manipulation, people will relay situations to you, because they would rather you do their dirty work while they hide their hands. To avoid being pulled into the battles of others, it's important to establish clear personal boundaries. Clearly define them and communicate them respectfully but assertively. Ask God to teach you how to show empathy without putting yourself in the position to become weighed down by the problems of others.

There are also battles that do not involve any type of conflict with others; these battles may come in the form of health, financial, certain losses, and more. These battles may have a direct impact on our quality of life and/or impact certain aspects of our future. When it comes to the battles that threaten our livelihood, we must pray and seek God's guidance on how to proceed. In the Bible, in 1 Samuel 30, when King David was facing trouble at Ziglag, his entire camp was invaded. His enemies captured the women as prisoners and took all of their goods and supplies. King David knew that his wife was also among the captives. Although very distressed, He chose wisdom. He paused and sought the Lord. He prayed and asked God if he should pursue his enemies, and the Lord provided Him with instructions. Because he showed utter dependence upon God and acted in wisdom, God gave Him victory, and he recovered all that was taken. This is a great reminder for us that seeking God's instructions should override emotional responses.

I'm amazed at King David's strength during one of his most difficult battles. It didn't just concern him; his entire camp was at the mercy of his enemies. Reading this biblical narrative, scripture tells us in addition to the women and goods being taken, the city was burned with fire. Furthermore, scripture says they wept until they had no more strength. Have you ever found yourself in a battle where you felt your entire strength was depleted? In my life, there have been countless moments where I believed I was doing the right thing, striving to lead a righteous life, yet felt overtaken by circumstances. Admittedly, doubt tried to consume me. However, I try to remind myself that challenges and tests are an inherent aspect of life. We have good days, and we have trying ones. When we are called to embark on significant endeavors for God, it is normal for challenges to occur. What truly counts during these times is our perspective regarding adversity. Sometimes I must remind myself that thinking my journey would be smooth sailing is futile. I also remind myself not to fall victim to the comparison trap. Yes, even for men, comparisons will enlist us in mental battles that will rob us of contentment.

There have been numerous instances when I questioned my faith. As a follower of Jesus Christ, I felt I should not have to grapple with many of life's tribulations. I even wondered if God truly loved me because I could not understand why I had to deal with heavy burdens. Before you snarl your nose at my truthfulness, allow me to encourage you by affirming that it is perfectly normal to harbor such doubts about the sovereignty of God. However, I am not advocating that anyone should question God's sovereignty, but there are moments in our lives when we inevitably wonder if He sees us. I recall the disciples wondering if Jesus knew they were in a storm while He slept. And if we were all honest, we would admit to having asked these questions at least once in our lifetime.

Believers know our authority and position in Christ. This knowing isn't to make us feel superior or that our faith somehow outshines another. It is to help us triumph and walk in victory through the various stages. There are some battles we can't pick. God chooses them for us. These battles refine our faith, build our resilience, and ultimately draw us into a more intimate relationship with Jesus Christ.

Despite these moments of doubt, I have never allowed my faith in God or His significance in my life to be eclipsed by the battles that loomed over me. As I wrote this chapter, I was reminded of the biblical story pertaining to the faith of David. In 1 Samuel 17, the Israelites faced the unsurmountable war against Goliath. Before David subdued him with the stones, He told the fearful army that the battle belonged to the Lord. Because He knew the battle wasn't his, he was merely the instrument used by God, he was assured of the victory. Therefore, do not rely on your own understanding, acknowledge God and He will direct your path.[1]

---

1   Proverbs 3:5-7 paraphrased

THERE IS SAFETY IN WISE COUNSEL

I encourage you to seek a mentor, preferably someone who can guide you toward your purpose. A mentor can help facilitate your journey from point A to point B, offering invaluable feedback and guidance. We all require someone to intercede for us and offer encouragement when we strive for purpose. A wise mentor, coach, or leader can offer a fresh perspective on your challenges. He or she will be instrumental in helping you see things from different angles and determine where to direct your focus. Drawing on their own experiences and knowledge, they may be able to provide insights on which battles are worth fighting and which ones do not align with your goals or values. They can also hold you accountable for your decisions and actions, ensuring that you stay focused on the battles that truly matter to your overall success and well-being.

When it comes to choosing a mentor, exercising wisdom and discernment is paramount. Selecting a mentor who aligns with your values and vision ensures that their guidance will enhance your personal, spiritual, and professional growth. Without a strong support system, constructive feedback, and honesty, it will be easy to give in to discouragement and or our own selfishness. I am deeply thankful for the mentors and individuals I believe have been divinely placed in my life. Their influence and guidance have shaped me into the husband, father, and servant of God that I am today. Through their wisdom and support, I have experienced transformative growth. Their mentorship has not only aided in my healing process but has also strengthened my faith and deepened my connection with God. Each encounter and shared experience has been a stepping-stone towards personal and spiritual evolution. One that underscores the significant impact the right Godly orchestrated mentor can have in a persons life.

In conclusion, we must choose battles wisely. Doing so is a profound strategy that transcends mere conflict resolution; it embodies a deeper understanding of self-awareness and strategic thinking. By embracing the wisdom of discerning when to engage and when to step back, individuals can navigate various challenges with grace and intelligence. Remember, every battle fought externally may or may not have the intended outcome. Ultimately, the journey of selecting which battles to fight effectively transforms conflicts into opportunities for growth and empowerment.

Prayer: *Heavenly Father, I am grateful for the insight you provide into my struggles. I humbly ask for discernment to recognize what I should hold onto and what, or whom, I should release. Please lead and guide me towards my purpose, and grant me the wisdom, strength, and hope necessary to endure my challenges. In Jesus' name, I pray. Amen.*

Take a moment to meditate and reflect. Write down what you feel God is speaking to you through this message.

76

CHAPTER EIGHT
A NEW MORNING

Today, something truly remarkable happened to me. I awoke with the weight of guilt and frustration from my actions in this Christian life lifted off me. Previously, I felt as if my mistakes were too many to forgive. It has been a challenging journey, and at times, I've found it hard to navigate through the situations I found myself in. I often believed I should be further along in life and on my spiritual journey. Although I am aware of my identity and whose I am, to be honest, I do not always measure up to the high standards of Christianity. (Bear with me, I will explain this in full detail in a few pages). I know many of you have felt or will feel this way at one point in life. We've heard it said, "When we know better, we do better." But we've all had moments when we've known better but failed to do better. The human inclination to self-protect and self-preserve can cause us to move from the foundations God outlined in His word. The truth is after I decided to move forward and follow hard after Christ, the new life I mentioned in Chapter 5 became heavy. I felt isolated and alone. I jumped in, and I do not regret my decision. It was the best thing I'd ever done. The issue came because I jumped without proper guidance. The Bible tells us that there is safety in a multitude of counselors. Because I wasn't surrounded by Godly counsel, I succumbed to the enemy's condemnation of my sins and mistakes. The new life was difficult for me to comprehend. God revealed a lot to me, and I was embracing my newfound identity. Yet the same voices from the past whispered failures and negativity. Even the sermons I heard became too heavy a burden as they caused me to sink into despair over my decisions and choices instead of fueling me with hope and a Savior whose grace was unlimited. To add insult to injury, when you've never known true love, believing that you are 1) loveable and 2), worthy of love is difficult to conceive. I've heard the saying, "It's lonely at the top." And never fully grasped that meaning, until the top, for me, was fully giving my life to Christ. The people I disconnected from also felt judged by me because my desires and appetite changed. I didn't want to be the same or be involved in the same things. It was no offense to them; it was a personal journey for me. A part of me was still struggling with acceptance, and not wanting them to be upset or feel judged, I once again caved into those emotions. I went to the same bars and hang-out spots to curtail the lonely days and nights. I'd long given up drinking, but to have companionship, brotherly conversations, and friends, I thought it would be ok to hang around even if I was not actively involved in what they were doing. I was recently divorced for the second time and gave in to loneliness and feelings of defeat. I re-entered the dating scene and entertained female companionships that I knew wasn't conducive to my purpose in God. Watching some of the TV shows and movies with them and their kids, the Holy Spirit convicted me as I sat staring at the screen. Silently, I beat myself up, wondering why was I there. To feel important, wanted, and needed, I once again subjected myself to things I knew would eventually slow my progress. I knew I had no desire to watch horror films or any film that did not bring glory to God. There was a battle going on between my flesh and my spirit. Before your jaw drops and your eyes bulge because of my choices, think about moments when you may be tempted to repeat a cycle of dysfunction, knowing full well that it will leave you feeling empty. I want you to fully comprehend this because what happened in my soul is not an isolated experience. I am generally quiet and keep to myself; however, as I openly share my journey with you, God is unmasking any hidden pride that would serve to protect me from criticism. It isn't easy to let people see your deficiencies; however, I find it better than cowering in shame or wearing a mask to pretend like I have it all together.

If you struggle with backsliding and returning to things from which God has removed from you, I want you to know that there's a new beginning waiting for you. You can revisit your path, recognize the lingering pain in your soul, and avoid compromising your values. That space isn't to guilt, shame, or embarrass you, but to offer you a new perspective and hope for moving forward. Moreover, when we come to Jesus Christ as we are, positional sanctification occurs the moment we receive Christ as our Savior. Which means He sets us apart to do His will. Progressive sanctification takes time. We progress as we move forward in obedience to God. It is synonymous with growing in God. Philippians 1:6 reiterates that God began a great work in us and is faithful to complete it. But I was like many of you who may feel as if you can't come to God just as you are. The enemy makes us feel too dirty, but God specializes in cleansing us. (Titus 3:5). Apostle Paul also knew this well. He states, "Not that I have apprehended, [am already perfect], but one thing I do, is forget those things which are behind and reach forward to the things that are before me. I press toward the mark for the prize of the high calling of God in Jesus Christ."

CHANGE BRINGS ISOLATION

When we do not understand isolation, it can be hard on our psychological state. It is easy to allow the enemy to plant false ideas and identities on us when we are in that place of purging out the old and learning to be steadfast and unmovable in the things of God. Fortitude, stamina, and being solid in God is the only way to combat the enemy. I failed and was overcome with guilt and depression. Guilt can be a place of remorse over wrongdoing, which prompts us to repent, but there is also improper guilt. This is the guilt that is produced when the devil weighs us down with the fact that we have sinned and fallen short despite God's forgiveness. Although I knew that God was merciful, I had yet to forgive myself. I put pressure on myself to present a certain image and when I fell back into the same patterns, I had a difficult time dealing with it. The enemy is conniving. He knows how to play on our emotions through our imaginations.

God tells us to bring our thoughts into captivity, and when

we do not do that, it gives the enemy the power to make us feel defeated. When we come to Christ, we tend to think our healing and wholeness will be instantaneous. In some ways they are, but lingering wounds and habits still need to be uprooted. God is so merciful that little by little He reveals to us what we need to do to be free. Think about it this way: If He simply zapped us clean, we would have no knowledge of what we need to work to stay free. In Psalms 119:71, King David said it was good that he was afflicted, because it revealed the Lord's decrees. A few verses before in v67, he says he went astray before he was afflicted, but now he obeys the Lord. This means without the pain of his disobedience, he would fail to see the seriousness of obedience to God.

Eventually, I saw that hanging out and entertaining women served as a distraction. It caused me to neglect my prayer and Bible study. I prioritized worldly pursuits over seeking God. I'm not making excuses for my backslidden behavior, but the truth is, we all fall short, and there is no yardstick for the magnitude of one's sins, and no sin is superior to another. Gossiping stands on equal footing with lying, stealing, idolatry, adultery, and even fornication. While the consequences may vary, they all fall under the umbrella of sin. I am not suggesting that these are the only sins people can commit; there are certainly more. I only highlight a few to emphasize that sin is sin.

I've also recognized that people will condemn you for fully following Christ and they will also seek opportunities to try to prove that you are not as "holy" as you say that you are. The enemy will attempt to derail us in any way that he can. He only has the power that we yield to him. God is all powerful and all dominion and authority belongs to Him. There are some key points to ponder in awakening to a new morning. When the clouds fade, and the sun rises, the Bible tells us that God's mercies are new every morning. His mercies allowed me to see that the period of isolation and aloneness didn't mean that He wasn't near. It was just the opposite. God is always near. So near that He wanted me alone so that He could confirm my call, reveal His plans and bring me closer in my walk with Him. In the isolation is also the refiner's fire. He wanted that time with me to purge me of everything that was unlike Him. Aloneness can be a test. What will you do when the walls seem to close in around you and the phone stops ringing? Where will you go when so-called friend's invitations cease? Additionally, even though you sometimes find the church home, you don't immediately find your tribe within the church. So, what do you do when satan whispers the Christian circle isn't as safe as you thought it would be? Isolation can cause you to question yourself, your call, and your abilities. Isolation and loneliness can overshadow everything you've worked to establish. Let's define them both, loneliness is the distressing feeling of being alone or separated. Isolation is the lack of social contact, and having few people to interact with regularly. [1]

Instead of giving in to the feelings and allowing the enemy to infiltrate your mind as he did mine, it is important to understand that God will allow you to be hidden to purge your

---

1   https://www.nia.nih.gov/health/loneliness-and-social-isolation/loneliness-and-social-isolation-tips-staying connected#:~:text=Loneliness%20is%20the%20distressing%20feeling,while%20being%20with%20other%20people. Accessed 03.20.24

character. Just as Jesus could do no miracles in His hometown because the people most familiar with Him did not believe, you, too, will face people who do not believe in you.

And although sin is sin, God does hold those with certain offices to a higher standard. (James 3:1). I mentioned earlier that I felt as if I couldn't measure up. As desires for the world and sin shift, the desire to please God becomes greater. I went backward then because somewhere in my soul, there was still the un-surrendered pain of a fragile and fractured man. One who was easily susceptible to spiritual and mental traps set up by the enemy. The enemy's seeds didn't haphazardly start, they went deeper than I realized into my childhood. Although I caved in those moments, I found my spirit and soul at war. I was inwardly battling my being in those places, because my spirit was quite disturbed. They did not bring the joy or comfort that I sought. My mind had been so clouded by the fear, disappointments, and shame that I wasn't able to see myself as God saw me. I was still acting out of hurt. It was my way of proving to myself and others that I was valuable.

Since my full release this time, I've walked in the grace of God that empowered me to stay away from negative thoughts and receive my deliverance. I recognize now God isolates us to protect us from corruption, and to sharpen the gifts He has given us by His holy Spirit. His chosen must be separated from the things that could negatively influence and compromise our integrity. The messages that He gives us to deliver, warn, correct, and edify others must come through that which is untainted. For example, John the Baptist lived in the wilderness. He was away from the societal norms of religion and politics. His isolation caused him to boldly proclaim that repentance was needed in the wake of the coming Messiah. We must change our perception of isolation to evolve into all that we are predestined to become. Isolation thus becomes a benefit more than a burden.

EVIL COMPANY CORRUPTS GOOD CHARACTER

God created us to dwell together in unity. In that unity, we must be careful that our association doesn't cause us to shrink from declaring what God conveys to us. Similarly, we find the prophet Elijah often needing rest from the crowds and the demands of ministry. God provided restoration and the strength he needed to continue his journey until his assignment was fulfilled. Likewise, with us, the period of isolation is the time that God uses to instruct us in His character, reveal the things that need healing, make us sensitive to His voice, and give us the zeal for the journey. I am the first to admit that silence can seem loud. However, it is in the quiet communion with God that I've been able to experience a deeper intimacy with Him. If we misidentify the isolation as rejection, we risk missing those God-taught moments.

I began this chapter with the "New Morning" because today I arose and God reminded me of a scripture from the book of Lamentations, which reads, "Through the Lord's mercies we are not consumed, because His compassions fail not. They are new every morning. Great is Your faithfulness" (Lam. 3:22-23 NKJV). Reading this scripture should ignite a sense of hope within each of us. Life presents numerous challenges, and we all make mistakes. However, knowing that each morning offers a chance for a fresh start can lift the burden of guilt and pressure that often weigh us down. Sadly, due to our lack of understanding, we allow the enemy and life's difficulties to relentlessly beat us down. We have a loving Father who forgives us, a Savior who died for us, and the Spirit of the living God dwelling within us. Thus, there's no room for defeat or depression in our lives. This does not mean that mental instability isn't real or that therapy and counsel aren't needed to overcome past trauma. Therefore, do not take this message as judgment or condemnation of your feelings. I in no way intend to minimize or trivialize them. As you've read, I've struggled with both. I am praying right now, as you retrace the paths that have led to your pain, that you, like me, would discover the truth that victory is found in Jesus Christ. His very nature is the framework that helps us to heal. He became the true motivation for me to know and do better. This profound revelation marked a turning point in my life. If I had not encountered the scripture in Lamentations, I might still be trapped in an old, defeated mindset, battling the same guilt and depression. I am grateful to God for looking beyond my faults and seeing who I am destined to be. In other words, He sees us for who we are in Him, not our present circumstances or mistakes. God desires the best for you; let me repeat that—God desires the best for you.

I stood at a critical moment; once again, I was faced with a decision: either remain in defeat or accept the fresh mercies and the grace being offered to me. I opted for the latter, and as a result, I now possess a renewed perspective and a brighter outlook on the grace of God. Thoughts control our behaviors, and the enemy will use them against us. That is why God admonishes us to think about things that are pure, lovely, holy, honest, true, and righteous. (Philippians 4:8). Changing our thoughts takes discipline. It is also liberating to understand that grace-the unmerited favor of God is not earned through performance; rather, it is a deliberate choice made by God to extend to us.

Let this message serve as a transformative moment for you. Understand that the blessings of love and grace you receive from our Heavenly Father are not based on whether you get everything right. They simply result from the love of God. I pray that you open your heart and let go of the burden of past failures. God's ways are higher than our ways and His thoughts greater than our thoughts. If you are willing to embrace the fresh mercies bestowed upon you each morning, and step into each day with a spirit of victory, there is still time to fulfill your purpose. There is still time for you to tap into the confidence and boldness that will reclaim everything the enemy has stolen from you and your bloodline! Perfectionism isn't the key to happiness; it is found in one's ability to remain teachable and humble enough to admit mistakes and grow from them. Before the foundations of the earth, God established your worth. No amount of time, mistakes, or rejection can alter that; they may threaten it but are incapable of changing it.

Prayer: *Father, help me to recognize areas in my life where I have not received your grace. Help me to let go of the need to be perfect and rest as you perfect me in your character. Please show me what I need to work on and how to walk in the revelation of your love* *and mercy. Lead me into a place void of distractions from guilt and mistakes and cause me to know that I am forgiven because of what Jesus did on the cross. Help me to let go of my past so that I may run this race unashamed in you. In Jesus name!*

Take a moment to meditate and reflect. Write down what you feel God is speaking to you through this message.

CHAPTER NINE
SECURING SPIRITUAL DOORS

As a man, I hold the solemn responsibility of ensuring the safety and security of my family. Night after night, my wife reminds me to check the doors, ensuring they are securely locked. This nightly ritual has been a constant throughout our marriage. Recently, I've discovered a profound lesson about it. While it may appear trivial to many, the truth is that open doors can serve as invitations, allowing anyone or anything to enter one's life. A door is not merely an object; it is a threshold or a boundary that separates you from what lies beyond it. This revelation holds profound significance, which God intends to communicate to His children. I find it genuinely remarkable when God speaks. I am consistenly amazed as it is often during unexpected moments and through ordinary things. These moments, when we least anticipate them, can be profoundly transformative and life-changing if we open our hearts to receive what God is communicating to us. The more we pray for understanding, the more attuned we become to His voice.

One day, after I arrived at work, a simple question unexpectedly crossed my mind, "Are your doors locked?" I took a moment to contemplate this, considering that I wasn't at home and my workplace had security measures. I remembered locking my car when I arrived at work, so I was uncertain which doors this question referred to. I pondered for a moment; then it dawned on me: perhaps it wasn't a reference to physical doors; instead, it alluded to my life's spiritual doors.

Doors can be entrances or exits. They can be a bridge to something great or a barrier. Since coming into knowledge and understanding of spiritual matters, I strive for consistency in all areas of my life. Which includes my choice of associations and the influences I allow through other measures. However, the more I meditated on doors, I found it to be an unmistakable sign that I needed to be vigilant. In the past, negative thoughts and lust came through doors that were opened because of my bloodline. Having closed them through repentance and renunciations, I'm typically cautious of what I entertain and who I allow into my intimate space. The enemy is subtle. Since God was speaking to me, I knew I needed to be more attentive. Social media opens us up to more than we can imagine. The wrong voice with the correct information is incredibly deceptive. We must spend time with God so that He can sharpen our spiritual discernment. The revelation struck me profoundly, particularly considering the ongoing spiritual battles we had been contending with.

Warfare is not uncommon for believers in Christ. But when things are intensified for no apparent reason, we must be sure that our atmospheres are purified. When my wife and I bought our home, everything was in place, and we were waiting for the closing date. A person from the lending company who was not assigned to our file made a mistake, which ended up causing us a lot of trouble. We had already sold the house we were living in and had to move out by a specific date. Because of the lender's error, we almost lost the deal. We had to come up with more money as a down payment for the new home, and we could have ended up homeless. Additionally, many other things were coming against us at the same time. As a result, fear, anger, frustration, and anxiety filled our minds and hearts. These things tormented us because we didn't know what we were going to do if the issue with the lender was not resolved in time. Ultimately, the situation worked out for us, and we could purchase and move into our home. Although we could breathe a sigh of relief at not being homeless, I harbored feelings of anger towards the lender. That situation was over, and we'd overcome that hurdle, but the feelings of bitterness lingered on.

As I've mentioned, life will offer us plenty of opportunities to face troubling emotions. Our emotions are not the problem. God gave them to us. They are a part of our wonderful human design. Our enemy seeks to set up strongholds and strongmen in our lives. It is difficult to always respond in faith in trying situations. However, we must guard our words, thoughts, and our hearts. The predisposed inclination towards sin makes it easier to react rather than act. We are not perfect, yet God calls us to walk in self-control.

I've learned to immediately go to God, even during tears, release the weight of burdens, and confess that He will make a way out of every negative situation. Depending on the severity of the trial, we must consistently release the weight and ask God to allow us to see the light in what appears dark. Romans 12:17 warns us to repay no one evil for evil. It further states, " Do things in such a way that everyone can see you are honorable." There was no way that I could have gotten revenge upon the lender who caused my wife and me undue stress and grief, but still, I allowed it to turn to bitterness in my soul. It was so bad that I couldn't find the joy to celebrate buying our new home. The enemy had completely stolen my focus and my peace. I believe two things happened in this situation. One was the enemy's trap that I'd fallen prey to, and the second was God revealing some deeply rooted issues that I had not dealt with.

The anger came in through doors that remained open to the enemy in my life. Understand that this revelation came because of the depth of the bitterness. Anger itself is not a bad thing. I want to clarify that so you will not believe everything that upsets you is the enemy. We are warned to be angry and not sin in scripture. (Ephesians 4:26-27). Let's examine it from the Amplified Bible because it gives a complete description. "Be angry [at sin—at immorality, at injustice, at ungodly behavior], yet do not sin; do not let your anger [cause you shame, nor allow it to] last until the sun goes down." We can be angry, but if the sun goes down while we are still angry, we've disobeyed God and opened the door for the enemy. According to this verse, we are to resolve matters quickly. Again, it is easier said that done. God will help us do what we feel incapable of doing in our own strength.   As I fervently prayed for understanding, I firmly believe that God revealed far too often, we inadvertently leave our spiritual doors unlocked, providing an open invitation for unwelcome influences and individuals to enter our lives without restraint. These intrusions can disrupt our existing peace and impede our path to success.

As I continued meditating on doors that morning at work, I remembered times during my youth when things beyond my control happened. Although I grew beyond those things, I had not disclosed nor dealt with them. Those secret matters were also doorways to anger, unforgiveness, and bitterness. Another thing that God brought to my mind was a period when I was selfish and ungrateful. My dad was doing the best to support us, although he and my mom divorced. I looked at what my friends had, like brand-new tennis shoes and video games. I wanted the attention from having new things as well. I wanted to feel important and validated. I disregarded that my sister's needs were more important than the material things I craved. She was graduating, and the senior fees could be costly, but in my young mind, I didn't understand why he "appeared" to make a difference between us. This may sound normal in the natural, but several doorways were opened in the realm of the spirit. Primarily covetousness, greed, selfishness, insecurity, and bitterness, to name a few. The more God reveals, even from the past, it is important that these sins be repented for and renounced by the Blood of Jesus. Spiritual doors affect more than one person; the entire bloodline can be affected and infected unless repentance is done. I lived several years angry at my father because I didn't get my way. Another thing I had to repent for was entitlement. Just because our parents are chosen to steward and provide for us, it doesn't mean they must cater to our every whim. In hindsight, I see how wrong my actions were. I was young and didn't realize the importance of simply conversing with my dad about it. In my childlike mind, I judged my father's love for me based on his failure to hand out money whenever I expected it. I allowed the enemy to plant false ideas about love, and as a result, I felt unloved by him. That seed started me on a downward spiral to find love and affirmation as I grew into adulthood. I sought validation from women and my close friends. A distorted view of love robs a person's identity and causes them to accept a lesser standard of true love. Because unforgiveness had already taken root in my youth, it was easy for me to walk through life being an unforgiving person. When my second ex-wife and I had issues, I was angry at myself for getting into the marriage. Although my dad passed away before this relationship, I was in that marriage, and the grief I felt compounded the already negative feelings that I was dealing with. I was bitter. Even though the relationship was broken before entering into it, the relationship was going downhill, and people consistently reminded me that I had made a huge mistake. I'm not here to bad mouth or discredit her because the fault lies with us. We married for the wrong reasons and couldn't have anticipated that we were both dealing with unhealed emotions and behaviors that were toxic. I will, however, state that her extreme jealousy made it difficult for us to live in harmony with one another and created a lot of tension with my family members. I hated my life at that point. The circumstances that I was in made me also dislike myself.

I felt that I should have known better and should have made better decisions. Therefore, I didn't treat the people in my life as well as I could have. The anger was debilitating. I now realize I had not forgiven myself for getting into these situations. When God tells us to forgive, He also indicates that we should forgive ourselves. Any form of unforgiveness is pride. Pride often blinds us to the true condition of our hearts. Because I had yet to purify my heart completely, I allowed unforgiveness and anger to fester. Isn't it just like God to bring things back to the surface so we can uproot them? He did this for me while sitting at my desk so that I could close the doors that remained open and hidden from anger, unforgiveness, and bitterness. It is a part of the regenerating work of the Holy Spirit and the purifying of our characters. Our ultimate goal is to be more Christ-like. I thought I was good. It wasn't that things were not going well, but God wanted me to be sure the perimeters around those areas were sealed shut. It also meant that I had to consistently cover my children so that the enemy would not find a gateway through the tiniest crack.

Additionally, I struggled with my dad passing away. I started drinking alcohol a lot more, although I was trying to live for God. The funny thing is, I didn't even like alcohol the same way that I used to. I had no desire to drink but thought I could somehow numb the pain. I used it as a coping mechanism and didn't realize that I was becoming more dependent on it than on God. The alcohol was another pun the enemy used to get me to revert to anger. I'm glad I chose to stop drinking. I find that not many of us understand the ramifications of opening doors to the enemy and how it will give him the legal right to inflict harm upon us and our entire bloodline. He used my vulnerability toward alcohol to interject intoxication into my future. He knew how easily my feelings could be hurt and how much negative thoughts would weigh upon me. I'm grateful to God to be in a place where my emotions no longer rule my actions. Because of the power of Jesus Christ, I could properly heal and process the past pain in my life. Once the doors were closed, I began to see the fruit of what God was doing in my life.

Concerning my dad, I felt the last two years of his life were the best years for him and me. Again, he wasn't a bad father at all. He was a great provider and always ensured that we did father/son things together. I missed the manly guidance and direction I needed early in life. I received discipline, but the intimacy between a father and son was missing. During his final years of life, in my adulthood, he conveyed his admiration, love, and joy for me as he saw me evolve into the man of God I was meant to become. His words broke years of bondage off my life and heart. In that instant, I felt like my spirit was finally able to soar.

I worked with him at his company, and he taught me a lot about the music industry. As a result, I am able to leverage what I learned from him and take my business to greater heights. That's just like God, to multiply the blessings through our seed! During these latter years, I also recognized how much God protected me and the image of my father, by allowing some distance between us. Because of God's mark on my life, He shielded me from any negative influences that could have impacted me before my dad gave his life to Jesus.

My heart rejoiced as my dad shared his testimony and love for Jesus before his passing away. God allowed me to see my dad as a man after His own heart. Our growing bond instilled in me traits of independence, hard work, and drive, yet it also made me hesitant to seek help when needed—Pride is another door the enemy uses to derail our paths.

THE DANGERS OF DEMONIC DOORS

Have you ever wondered why everything appears to be sailing smoothly, only to suddenly find yourself confronted by unexpected challenges that seemingly materialize out of thin air? These challenges can rear their heads at the most inconvenient and vulnerable junctures in our lives. When we neglect to secure doors from our past, we unwittingly subject ourselves to the influence of those things that seek to pull us back into a place from which God has already delivered us. To put it plainly, the wrong spiritual doors threaten our future. If we do not close them and keep them shut, we risk forfeiting great seasons of our lives by delaying our destiny.

Further reflections led me to recall when I reopened doors in my life after finally marrying my purpose partner and wonderful wife. I reconnected with old friends, some of whom I realized were designed to pull me back into lifestyles I'd broken free from. I was judged because there were things that I no longer desired, like drinking or partying. Returning to the same environment indicated that my identity was still in a crisis. The part of me that never wants to hurt people and always makes others happy [people pleasing] resurfaced. Although I was no longer in the same place and didn't feel I could relate to former acquaintances, when I received invitations, I hesitated to turn them down. Therefore, I tried to entertain them, but it created a war within me and added conflict in my life where there was peace. I've learned in seasons of life, you advance by moving ahead, even if that means you do so without certain individuals. The word "No" has been liberating. Keeping wrong associations also opens doors to unnecessary problems. I have a beautiful family and cannot afford to damage the people that I am responsible for. I got the revelation, "It's bigger than me." Therefore, when deciding to choose associations, I must also consider the impact it will have on my family. Leaving doors unlocked can inadvertently give the enemy unrestricted access to your life. Our ultimate goal is to advance toward the promises that God has laid out for us. To accomplish this, we must wholeheartedly permit Him to seal these doors, thereby ensuring that our future remains impervious to anything or anyone not divinely appointed to be part of it.

In conclusion, let us all be vigilant in examining and securing the doors of our lives, both physically and spiritually. Doing so protects our present and future from unnecessary turmoil and setbacks. Remember, just as we lock our homes for safety, we must also yield to God's hand in locking our spiritual doors to safeguard our hearts and destinies. As I pen these words, I offer a heartfelt prayer that our eyes may be opened, aligning with the wisdom of Ephesians 1:18 (KJV), enabling us to discern which doors require closure and locking. I wholeheartedly encourage you to pray, earnestly seeking God's divine guidance to identify and firmly close these doors. Not only your well-being but also that of your family hinges on this crucial act.

Prayer: *Father, you can open and close doors in my life. If there is any door that I am keeping open, which you have granted me the ability to close, please reveal it to me and enable me to close it. Grant me insight and foresight regarding anything or anyone I may be holding onto that I need to remove from my life. I no longer want to hinder myself from stepping into everything you have prepared for me. Help me lay aside every weight and sin that will easily beset me; in Jesus' name. Amen!*

Take a moment and write down what you feel God is speaking to you in this moment.

CHAPTER TEN
AWAKEN TO DIVINE DEPENDENCE

One of life's most challenging situations is finding oneself in a place where the presence of God seems absent. This false reality creates a disheartening delusion in the minds of many individuals. Amid feeling as if God is absent, some sorrowfully have negated the need for a savior altogether. It is unsettling to realize that society has subtly conditioned us to lead lives detached from God's guidance. However, it is crucial to underscore that we were not designed for independence from our Creator; our very purpose is to worship Him with the depths of our hearts, the entirety of our minds, and the fullness of our souls. While a degree of independence is not negative, we must guard against an arrogant mindset.

My most fulfilling days are those when I wholeheartedly depend on God for everything. I once experimented with life on my terms and soon realized that living according to God's plan was undeniably better. My way left me feeling empty, guilty, frustrated, defeated, negative, and lonely. I experienced firsthand what it means to want things to happen fast. I compared my life to my acquaintances and through pride, I felt inadequate. Strangely, pride reveals itself when we least expect it. When most of us think of pride, we think of boasting or arrogance, however; it is also expressed when our emotions have mastery over us. I mentioned learning about a book by Rhonda Byrne titled, *The Secret* in a previous chapter. I was selling cars in Indiana, and my sales manager introduced me to it. I was very vulnerable at the time and the more I entertained his conversation, he was able to get into my head. I had faith and loved God, but my mind was focused on getting ahead. Honestly, I was tired of waiting. I'd grown weary watching others move into their area of promise, and my life still seemed stagnant. It wasn't that I didn't have money; I wanted more. I also wanted to drive a luxury vehicle to prove my worth. The funny thing is, God will always correct us when we veer too far off course. Without realizing it, I'd embraced and tempted to employ the methods outlined in *The Secret* to manifest my desires. Manifestation is the theory that we have the power to control our own destiny, desires, and dreams. Apart from the practices of manifestation, God has given us the ability (creativity, genius, know-how to get wealth). When we add unbiblical meditation, focusing intently on our desires every day, calling them in by repetition or other means, we are crossing the lines into witchcraft. The practice of manifestation and law of attraction also puts our will ahead of God's will. The Bible says that His ways are higher than ours, and His thoughts are not ours. (Isaiah 55:8-9) The most dangerous thing about the practice of manifesting is idolatry. When our own desires and will become our focus, we are in danger of unknowingly giving them our worship. In manifestations, we are also looking to ourselves and not God. He commands us to lean not to our own understanding; rather, we are to acknowledge Him in all of our ways. As we do this, we trust Him to guide us. Another danger in using manifestation is to totally disregard God. Many manifestation gurus use scriptures from the Bible and pray to include Him, but their hearts, intentions and motivations are wrong. Deuteronomy 8:17-18 says, "Beware lest you say in your heart, 'My power and the might of my hand have gotten me this wealth.' You shall remember the Lord your God, for it is he who gives you the power to get wealth, that he may confirm His covenant that he swore to your fathers, as it is this day."

The enemy loves to answer unrighteous prayers and grant desires. That is his way of deceiving people into turning their worship away from God. I'm glad God revealed this to me before I could get too deep into it. God checked me and told me what I was doing was demonic and I repented and got back in line. I remember praying and confessing that I didn't want anything if it did not come from God. I want all He has for me, but I want it in His timing. I know when He grants everything, it will give Him glory, and I am able to properly steward it well.

In spiritual warfare, manifestation is merely one strategy in the adversary's arsenal to estrange us from our divine dependance on God. He is crafty and strategically lies to us by sowing seeds of doubt concerning God's benevolence towards us. He boldly insinuates that our loyalty hinges primarily on the grace and favor we receive. Just as he dared to challenge the steadfastness of Job, a model of faithfulness in the Bible, he issued similar charges against us. The enemy's insidious aim is to test whether our devotion to God is unwavering even in the face of adversity, questioning if we serve out of pure love or mere self-interest.

Despite being stripped of his riches, health, and comfort, Job's faith remained resolute. He sets the example of what it means to be steadfast in the refusal to denounce allegiance to God. Though Job was unwavering in his devotion to God, even he fell into the trap of vulnerability and pride. Extreme pain can cause us to lose sight of God. However, the restoration in his life was far greater than what he'd lost. Delve into the profound book of Job when the opportunity arises. It will give witness and encourage you to stand strong amidst life's most grueling trials. During my own moment of weakness, I'd unknowingly embraced the falsehood that I could attain all my desires without God. In my error, I perceived myself as a good person and thought I deserved everything that I was attempting to manifest, including the Bently.

Regrettably, my definition of being a "good person" was flawed and the principles proved inadequate. It became evident that my own summation of goodness fell short of the standards instilled within me by God. The thing we learned about demonic doorways in the previous chapter is that one open doorway to the enemy is often followed by another. Pride is sneaky and subtle. I allowed it in through my emotions. It grew as I attempted to manifest my own desires, and I arrogantly thought I deserved the material things I wanted. It wasn't that I didn't work hard for the things I wanted, however, manifestation is a lazy way of obtaining them. Proverbs 13:4 says, "Lazy people want much but get little, but those who work hard will prosper." Simply putting things on a vision board, without working to obtain them is laziness. I'm all for writing your vision and keeping your goals in eye view so that you do not lose sight of them, but working to achieve them is key. Let's look at the demonic doorways that I allowed to be open over my life through my ignorance and faulty emotions. Coveting led to pride, which led to idolatry. This was no small thing, so I don't want you to make light of it. Among the seven things God hates most are pride, lust, greed, and sloth. (Proverbs 6:16). All of these sins are intertwined. The lust for more turns into greed and pride. Eventually, the desire becomes so strong that it is easy to do whatever it takes to obtain it even if it leads us away from God. The root is always *idolatry*. This is another reason the Bible tells us to keep our eyes single without distraction.

Of the thirty-eight parables Jesus tells, sixteen deal with the subject of money.[1] He emphatically teaches that happiness and joy are not found in the abundance of things. Before I finish on the parables of Jesus, let's look at Matthew 19:16-24. In summary, a man came to Jesus and asked him what he must do to gain eternal life. Jesus told him to obey the commandments. He thought to himself and happily shared the commandments he'd kept. He thought surely, he was destined for eternal life. But Jesus hit him where it hurt. He told him to sell everything he owned and give the proceeds to the poor, and then follow Him.

---

1 Idelman, Kyle. "Jesus Is My Provider." Gods at War, Zondervan, Grand Rapids, MI, 2013, pp. 167–167.

The man went away sad for he had acquired many possessions and had great wealth. This showed the idol in his heart was his wealth.

While teaching a large crowd, before the parable of the "rich fool" a man in the crowd tells Jesus to command that his brother give him a part of his inheritance. Jesus refused by asking who made him arbiter between them. Then, Jesus seizes the opportunity to teach about greed and pride, turns to the crowd, and says, "Watch out! Be on guard against all kinds of greed; life does not consist in an abundance of possessions."

He also taught that no one could serve two masters. It is impossible to give wholehearted devotion to God and other things. Life consists of balance. However, God must be first. I am not where I desire to be; however, nothing can replace the happiness or contentment that I have in my heart. My wife and I have acquired many things, and we do have financial aspirations, but our primary goal is pursuing Jesus Christ. We have dedicated our lives to His service and fulfilling His call and purpose.

Jesus warns us about Mammon. It's the god of money. The problem is, that the more you feed this idol, the more it grows. It becomes bigger and bigger until it is all-consuming. It's like the more you have, the more you want. It will never be enough. Don't get me wrong, wealth is not evil. We need money to build and help others. We must still walk circumspectly to guard our hearts. It's the love of money that is the issue.

A JEALOUS GOD

You shall not make for yourself an [idol], in the form of anything. You shall not bow down to them or worship them; for I, the Lord your God, am a jealous God. The weird thing about idolatry is that it doesn't have to be a person, statue, or image. The sneaky idols are always the ones we set up in our hearts. Idols can be family, a career, money, sex, etc. It is whatever takes our devotion, time, attention, and focus too far away from God. Exodus 34:14 reads, "Do not worship any other god, for the LORD, whose name is Jealous, is a jealous God."

It's uncanny for people to think of God as jealous. How could He be jealous of His children? This is where we have understood God to be like us-merely human. We tend to get jealous "of" others. God cannot be reduced to our finite level. He is jealous "for" us. "And here's what is said of God: "For the Lord your God is a consuming fire, a jealous God" Deuteronomy 4:24. God knows what our independence from Him will do to us. He knows how easy it is for us to be seduced by the enemy, and out of love for us, He places boundaries to protect us. He is jealous or rather zealous for our futures. Zeal is defined as extreme enthusiasm and passion. We can see how jealousy is tied to it. God is so extremely passionate (in love) with us that He sent His Son to die for us. Therefore, God's jealousy is not only indicated by His abhorrence of sin, but it is demonstrated in His pursuit of us. God demonstrated His love for us in this, while we were still sinners, Christ died for us. (Romans 5:8)

Although God pursues us, at times, it is easy to forget

about Him. It saddens me to think that there was ever a time in my life that I didn't consider God. That's how idolatry works in the life of the believer. It's not always bowing to an image; it's bowing in your heart. Most of the time, it happens before we even think about it, because we are so caught up in achieving, thriving, and doing that we forget about God. Again, it's not done intentionally. It just happens. Like God's chosen people. Isaiah 30 tells us they sought comfort, and provision, without consulting God. He said they carried out plans that were not His. They formed alliances (connections) undirected by His Spirit. He even mentions they sought Pharaoh's protection and shade for refuge without His guidance. God is serious about our dependence upon Him. He isn't trying to control us; His motivation is always for our highest good. (Jeremiah 29:11)

When we embrace His love for us, we will also trust His guidance, provision, and protection. If we depend exclusively on our personal morals and personal talents, we often find ourselves bending them to align with our ideologies and convenience. This will cause us to lack the conviction of the fundamental morals and standards set by our heavenly Father. Without conviction, we remain blind to our errors. Spiritual blindness hinders the opportunity to repent and transform our behavior.

It may be tempting to ignore the conviction in our hearts, but doing so only keeps us in bondage. One of the most crucial aspects of depending upon God is our freedom and deliverance. Psalms 37:40 says, "The Lord helps them and delivers them because they take refuge in Him." Again, this cautions us to seek refuge in our savior. Our safety net isn't in careers, jobs, or our spouses; it is in God. He tells us to delight in Him, and He will give us our heart's desires. Let's examine Psalm 37:4 in detail; because of pride and self-indulgence, we often focus on the latter part of this verse, again putting our desires ahead of God. Vs 4 is peppered in the middle of trusting in the Lord, Vs.3, and committing our ways to Him in Vs. 5. How strategic is our God! Putting our trust in God will lead us to delight (find peace, satisfaction in, rejoice in Him). The Hebrew word for delight means to "be soft, delicate, dainty, and happy."[2] This delicate process involves focusing our eyes on Him in every circumstance. Being delicate means our hearts are pliable and moldable. Thus, we find our strength and daily delight in Him. Actively seeking God and cultivating a personal relationship with Him is key to receiving His desires for us. This is contrary and controversial to what most believe and have been taught about this verse. Most prosperity gospel messages use it to prod people into putting prosperity above anything else. The truth is, ….."and He will give you the desires of your heart." In this verse, the heart means the inner man, mind, and will.[3] Let's tie it all together: Delight (being delicate and pliable enough for Him to mold us into the image of His Son). We become more like Him, and His desires replaces the sinful, self-centered, selfish, desires of our hearts. The former desires were born out of coveting, insecurities, lusts of the flesh and the pride of life.

God created us. He knows us better than we know ourselves; therefore, He will give us the things we need. In contrast to the method of manifestation and prosperity gospel centered

2   https://biblehub.com/hebrew/6026.htm
3   https://biblehub.com/hebrew/3820.htm

messages, our delighting in God, puts the focus on the Giver-who is God. We aren't coming to Him with a list or showing Him our vision boards, we don't ask amiss. We are told to ask according to His will, and He promises to answer. (1 John 5:14-15)

I have journeyed alongside God for most of my life, and it has been an adventure filled with trials that led to a profound sense of fulfillment. God has chosen to work through me, to touch countless lives. And what makes this journey incredibly beautiful is that all the glory goes to Him. I recognize my need for Him. I am totally dependent upon Him. The oxymoron is, while I am everything, He says that I am; I am absolutely nothing without Him. And while it might seem like there are countless rules, it is crucial to differentiate between mere religious practices and the depth of a personal relationship with God. Dependence upon God first begins with what Jesus commanded of us, "the denial of self." (Matthew 16:24). Denying self is not an easy thing to do. It makes us care less about our own reputations, defending our names, personal comforts, and the need to be right. In a culture filled with a generation that wants the right to be heard and validated, this will be a challenge. In fact, it is a daily test for each of us. God isn't asking us to mask our feelings; He is asking us to evaluate them. Ask yourself, Do I want to speak my mind to gain some sort of advantage, recognition, or feelings of self-worth or importance? Do I need to prove my point or my side? Am I trying to prevent feelings of humiliation about where I am or what I have?

Dying to self is less about us and more about embracing the

will of God. It isn't optional for Christians. The old way of life, must be obliterated with its former tendency to sin. This is part of the sanctifying work of the cross. The death of Jesus Christ made us alive with Him. We are no longer dead in our trespasses but have new life in Christ. This new life is our new covenant. With the same zeal that we pursued our sinful desires, we must now pursue that which pleases God. In essence, dependence upon God is the highest level of humility. We are not our own. We were bought at a price. Remember this truth: Living without God is impossible, as our very essence relies entirely on Him.

Prayer: *Father, please help me become wholly dependent on You in every aspect of my life. Let me not choose independence from You while leaning on the systems of this world. Forgive me and have mercy on me for the areas where I have fallen short. I humbly submit myself before You. Thank You for Your never-ending grace. In Jesus' name, Amen!*

Take a moment to meditate and reflect. Write down what you feel God is speaking to you in this moment.

CHAPTER ELEVEN
ACHIEVING GREATNESS

Greatness starts within, then it is projected outwardly. If it starts with outward success, the character to sustain the outer success will be absent. Developing character is the essential bedrock of all success. Nearly everyone wants to achieve a level of success or greatness. I said nearly everyone because some people are comfortable where they are, even if they haven't reached their full potential. The lackadaisical approach to life can be attributed to many different factors. e.g., environment, under-achievers in the family, the poverty spirit, and low self-worth to name a few. Before attaining my dream job and coming into the awareness of my own greatness, I mentioned before how much I struggled with my confidence and self-esteem. Although I fought inward battles, I always knew there was more to life than I was currently living. I knew the potential inside of me, but struggled with the fact that not everyone recognized or applauded me for it.

During seasons of hardship and not having those around you to celebrate and affirm your worth, it is easy to become envious of those who seem to be thriving. Observing others in their element when ours seem to be on hold, can cause us to wonder what steps they took to get to where they are? Honestly, bitterness and resentment can creep up as we wonder why not us? There is a lot to unpack about this topic. But before we get into that, we must first define greatness. If we do not have a clear definition of what it means to achieve greatness, we will find ourselves going in circles the same way a dog chases its tail.

I believe greatness is accomplishing all that God has created for us to do. The process and the level of success may look different for everyone, however, most of the principles are the same. Both terms, greatness and success, can be used interchangeably. The definitions can depend upon the individuals seeking to achieve them. When we think of success, perhaps, we look at a person who earns six figures, or a business whose revenue shows a million dollars. We also look at the fame and/or perhaps the number of followers in today's world of the "influencer" culture. However, success and greatness exist beyond the bottom line on a financial statement. If greatness isn't achieved on the inside first, all other avenues of it will eventually crumble.

The Bible says, "We are fearfully and wonderfully made" (Psalms 139:14). But what does this mean? I believe what the writer is conveying to the readers is that God paid special attention to the way He created us. In reviewing the Hebrew meanings of the words fearfully and wonderfully made, they mean to be in awe at our distinction and uniqueness. In fact, when we keep reading in that same verse, the writer goes on to convey that God's works are marvelous! The word marvelous in the Hebrew bears reference to extraordinary. Let's look a little deeper into our English dictionary; the word marvelous means astonishing and miraculous.[1] From this one verse, God is telling each of us that we were created with such unique detail that we should be in awe at how wonderful we really are. It is unfortunate that our greatness can get diminished or overshadowed by how we allow others to define us. Other times, our light is dimmed by our own failure to tap into the greatness we possess. Jeremiah 1:5 says that God knew us before He formed us in our mother's womb. How amazing is it to know God knew every detail about us, and every proclivity we would have toward sin, yet He chose to love us and bring us into the world. Because greatness is the essence of who God is, and because we bear His image, He had specific purposes and assignments for us to accomplish in the earth. The late Dr. Myles Munroe said the graveyard had the most treasure. By failing to tap into the greatness inside of them, it died along with them.

It is easy to squander time trying to figure out what you were created to do by comparing yourself to others instead of seeking God for His plan for your life. Comparisons can create a false or pseudo-identity. When you try to mold yourself into what someone else is doing or try to attain the things they have,

---

1   https://www.merriam-webster.com/dictionary/marvelous

you can cause yourself to forfeit the victory and great things that God has in store for you.   The entire biblical narrative of David offers much to the life of the reader by way of encouragement, leadership, failures, mistakes, and more importantly his heart for God and worship. In chapter 17 of 1 Samuel, we find a story most of us learned in children's church or Sunday school— The story of David and Goliath. I mentioned this briefly in the previous chapter, but we will go into a bit more depth in this chapter.

I found this story fascinating as a child and more intriguing as I delved deeper into scripture as an adult. Take a brief journey of this crucial moment in biblical history with me for a second. As chapter 17 begins, the Philistines assembled themselves for war against the Israelites. The Philistines were in constant conflict with Israel because they sought ownership of the land that God promised to His people Israel. They were also known for their advanced weaponry and military might. As Goliath, who the Bible describes as a giant, came forward for battle, he tormented Israel with threats. Goliath was not only a giant, but the Bible also describes his muscular stature and the heavy armor that he wore. Knowing they were no match for Goliath, even King Saul, the King of Israel, trembled with fear. Imagine an entire army afraid of one man! Picturing him, I can see a giant like King Kong or something, who is able to wipe out entire cities with one swoop! In that case, I can certainly understand the fear. The Bible describes 40 days of taunting by Goliath. He stood on the battle line bullying the army of the Lord. David's older brothers were in the army and stationed for battle; however, David was still young and had never enlisted in the army. He was back home away from the battle taking care of his regular sheep herding duties. His father wanted him to take food and supplies to the soldiers and his brothers who were stationed at the Valley of Elah. As David approached the place where the commander and the army were positioned, he noticed the army was unable to advance forward and heard the threats from Goliath. He could sense their distress and inquired as to what was going on. But his brothers basically told him he was being prideful and nosey and encouraged him to go back to tending sheep.

Allow me to inject right here, be careful of those people who only see you in what you were formally operating in. Your circle matters. The reality is that people will have a hard time seeing you operating in greatness. Now back to David, he rose up in boldness and said that he'd take on Goliath by himself. How could a mere shepherd boy with no battle experience rise and want to defend the army of the Lord? It was the heart of God within him. He knew no matter how great the obstacle was, with the power of God on the inside of him and faith in God, he could never be defeated. King Saul, at the time, loved David. Therefore, when he heard that he'd come down he immediately sent for him. David expressed his heart to defeat Goliath, but King Saul hesitated to allow it. However, David ignored all the negativity and finally convinced the King to permit him into battle. There are several lessons here. First, we see that David had to ignore the negative talk, discouraging words, and the lack of other people's belief in his abilities. Second, he remained focused on what was in his heart to accomplish. As we go further in the story, King Saul wanted to arm David with his personal armor and helmet. The amour didn't fit David. It wasn't created for him. He chose to refuse the armor of King Saul. The third lesson for us is, just as David could not accomplish his mission in something that was not designed for him, we cannot fulfill the call of God on our lives with someone else's armor (vision).

The Bible says that David had five smooth stones. He defeated Goliath with one. Why did David have 5 five stones? The King James Version of 2 Samuel 21:18-22, mentions a brother of Goliath. Think about it for a moment. David was prepared for any unforeseen obstacles. While Goliath's brother didn't pose any immediate threat, there was always the possibility of him joining in the fight. Not to mention, with the size of Goliath, David had to be prepared for anything.

Furthermore, if David would have been weighed down with Saul's armor, instead of what God equipped him with, the story might have ended differently. Defeating Goliath with what God gave him, brought him great success and changed the trajectory of his life. This was a part of God's plan and everything he went through prior to this moment proved to prepare him for success. The final lesson from this biblical narrative is, greatness happens when we are prepared through ordained processes.

STRATEGIZING FOR SUCCESS

It is key to seek God for strategy in everything you do. Proverbs 3:5-7, tells us to trust God with all our heart and lean not on our own understanding but in everything acknowledge him and He will direct our paths. Leaning on our own understanding hinders us from accomplishing what God called us to do. The reality is that we have been in this world and have picked up some falsehoods along the way. There are so many tutorials on how to become a millionaire that sound convincing. However, the steps that work for one may not work for all. People buy into them, not realizing they are making the person selling the information rich, while they are stifled in their own growth. I'm not saying that the paths that others have taken do not have merit and can't give us wisdom. The Bible says that we overcome by the blood of the lamb and the word of our testimony. Our testimonies and journeys can benefit one another through encouragement and empowerment, yet someone else's story cannot override God's purpose and plan for your life. Therefore, vision must be known. When we have a vision for our own lives and understand our own purpose, it will keep us from denying our own greatness. In John 18:37, Jesus said, "For this reason I was born, and for this I came into the world, to testify to the truth." Jesus had a clear vision for His life. Although there were those in His circle who did not fully understand his mission, He didn't allow their unbelief to get Him off course. As you seek God's will for your life, you will be more inclined to accept the greatness God has put within you.

I understand that life can make you feel like greatness is far away, and achieving purpose is hard to grasp. It's frustrating to wake up every day and not see your dreams realized, but be fully persuaded that if God gave you the vision, He will bring it to pass. If you dwell in self-doubt, you must ask yourself, "Who have you given a voice in your life? Whose words have you considered above Gods? And or perhaps it is complacency that has you in a place of stagnation. Have you settled for less than you deserve because you have grown comfortable? Purpose will ignite passion. Make no mistake about it, there will be no fulfillment of purpose without the passion and zeal to accomplish it! Ecclesiastes 9:10 says, "Whatever your hand finds to do, do it with all your might." Therefore, hard work is another essential element for forging ahead towards purpose. Remember your purpose isn't what you do for you; it is what you do for God and will leave indelible footprints in the world for future generations.

In review, achieving greatness first comes through understanding that God is the Source of greatness. When we think of His inexhaustibleness, and how Awe-Inspiring He is, we can rest in the fact that we are in His image. Next, we must accept that obstacles will come regardless of how hard we strive to do right and live our lives to the best of our abilities. Life is an ongoing series of trials and adversities; it is the nature of our journey. After all, when you are called to achieve greatness, should you really expect an easy path? Did you think it would be handed to you on a silver platter? Perhaps this is why you have experienced disappointment. It is important to understand that greatness is not an entitlement. While greatness may reside within you, it will still require diligent effort to discover and attain it. The most remarkable achievements in life rarely come without persistent dedication. I must confess, although I knew I would someday achieve great things, I didn't have definable boundaries. Neither did I set precise things in place, instead I lived under the shadow of what I saw in others. It was liberating for me to walk in my own greatness.

In the previous chapter, we discussed the power of choosing your battles. I must reiterate the importance of focusing your attention on the things that will propel you closer to greatness. If something is not contributing to your ultimate purpose, it is likely detracting from it. Often, we invest too much energy into frustrating situations that are beyond our control. In such instances, it is crucial to shift our focus towards the things we have power over. The issues we cannot alter must be entrusted to God through prayer. Have faith, pray when necessary, and act when needed. Do not lose hope simply because obstacles come your way. Remember, when Peter tried to talk Jesus out of going to the cross, he was rebuked. When the weight of what He was about to undergo became heavy, Jesus asked that if there was any other way than the excruciating pain of the cross, He still proclaimed, "none the less, not My will but thy will be done" (Luke 22:42). Have you determined that your path is yours alone, and your destiny will be fulfilled no matter what? That's the stern mentality and resolve you will need to achieve your highest self and impact the world around you.

Lastly, achieving greatness often demands sacrifices, but in the end, it will be well worth it. Refuse to be bullied by your limitations. Fight back through prayer, fight back with hope, and refuse to let life beat you down to the point where your dreams of greatness fade. Keep pushing forward until you reach your destination. I reiterate, bless God, and keep moving forward!

Remember, God will equip you to do everything that He created you to do. Greatness can never be realized in the bed of mediocrity. You were designed for more! I've outlined some principes below to help you develop action steps for fulfilling your purpose.

Prayer must be a Priority: Your relationship with God will sustain, guide, and direct you toward greatness.

Identify and Clarify: You must have a clear vision for your life and future. What is God calling you to accomplish? What talents and gifts do you possess? Refine them and develop a clear plan. Refine what you need to achieve your goals.

Connection: The Bible teaches us that evil company corrupts good character. Have you assessed your inner circle?

Count the Cost: Make wise investments in developing your character, mindset, and vision.

Embrace Challenges: Understand that obstacles are a natural part of life's journey, especially when you aspire to achieve greatness. Do not be discouraged by difficulties; instead, view them as opportunities for growth.

Practice Patience: Patience will deepen your faith in God as you work towards your goals.

Shift your Perspective: Reframe disappointments as valuable learning experiences. Greatness is not handed to anyone on a silver platter. It requires persistent effort and dedication.

Prioritize Purpose: Focus on what truly matters in your life and your pursuit of greatness. Determine which battles align with your purpose and will propel you forward while letting go of distractions that hinder your destiny.

Trust in Faith: When faced with challenges you cannot control, place your trust in a higher power through prayer. Maintain your faith and believe that things will work out for the better.

Maintain Hope: Regardless of the chaos around you, keep hope relevant. Remember that challenges are not surprising to God, and they should not surprise you either.

Persist in Perseverance: Understand that setbacks and deviations from your plans do not equate to failure. They simply mean you have more ground to cover on your journey towards greatness.

Sacrifice for Success: Acknowledge that achieving greatness often demands sacrifices. Be prepared to invest the time, effort, and resources necessary to reach your goals.

Stay Resilient: Be relentless in pushing forward towards your dreams of greatness.

Keep Moving Forward: In times of doubt or chaos, remember to thank God and keep moving forward. The journey may be challenging, but with persistence and faith, you can overcome any obstacle and reach your purpose.

Prayer: *Dear God, I seek your divine wisdom to understand all that You have orchestrated for my life. I trust Your plans and delight in Your will. I ask you to forgive me for times that I've doubted my own abilities and doubted that You would bring my dreams to pass. I place my trust in You. I commit to Your will for my life and dedicate the talents, resources, and gifts You have given me to You, to use as You will. I ask You to multiply them for Your glory. I prophecy that I can do all things because it is You who strengthens me. I am fortified by the Blood of Jesus to accomplish great things. I embrace all that You have for me. In Jesus' name, Amen*

Take a moment to meditate and reflect. Write down what you feel God is speaking to you through this message.

125

CHAPTER TWELVE
UNFAILING LOVE

For as long as I can remember, I wanted to be loved. After all, it is our basic human need. When that need goes unmet or is distorted by false perceptions of love, the burden for it becomes idolatry. Strangely enough, we can make our longing desires and immense needs become idols. These idols captivate our hearts causing us to devalue ourselves, undermine our own worth, and settle for less than we deserve. I found myself searching for love and fulfillment in people who were incapable of feeling the voids in my heart. Don't get me wrong, some of the voids were valid. And some were created in my mind, because of the insecurities I had. The enemy starts early making sure that our minds are filled with negative thoughts about ourselves. He will employ our relatives, friends, and even our parents to speak words that are harmful. At times we are also victims of acts like molestation and rape. He will do whatever it takes to ensure our demise. But God! Because of His great love for us. His plans always outrank the enemy's plans.

Throughout this book, you've journeyed with me through the pain of my past. We've discussed the insecurities and low self-image. I've written how I falsely perceived my father's unwillingness to cater to my every whim as a lack of love. And it's true, anytime we feel unloved, we are in danger of also feeling unlovable. We will think something is wrong with us; that we are not good enough. It will leave us fighting to prove our worth; a worth that we don't really know. Because we can't see our own value, regardless of the effort we expend, we will always come up short. I remember trying to gain weight as the haunting memories of being bullied for being tall and skinny replayed in my mind. It didn't work out for me. I'm well beyond that childhood age and I am still of a thin frame. The wonderful thing is, I've learned to accept and love who I am. The people who couldn't see my value back then, had power over me, because I also failed to see my own value. As I grew and entered dating relationships, I found myself always trying to rescue people. That level of co-dependency also came from the distorted views I had about love. Being the "fixer" caused me to think that I was needed. However, the people didn't need me, on the contrary, I needed them. It took a while for me to realize it, but the signs were there. I'd sacrifice myself for others who weren't worthy of the sacrifice, which led me to being taken advantage of. I'm not writing to play victim. I'm sharing my truth so that if you recognize these behaviors within yourself, you will have the tools and empowerment to overcome and change them. Unfortunately, it is the ridicule and judgment of others that keeps men from being emotionally available for themselves and for others. However, allowing God to heal you, will release you from their opinions.

I wasn't the most popular kid in school and bullying caused me to retreat into isolation. As I grew into my teenaged years, I wanted to be accepted by my peers and to date like everyone else. The young girls that I had crushes on didn't feel the same way about me. They thought that I was too skinny and unattractive. Imagine the ego of a young man being crushed by rejection. It changed my self-perception. The enemy slowly robbed my esteem and my self-worth. I felt devalued and it carried over into my adulthood. It is very difficult to date someone who is broken. Keep in mind, that brokenness doesn't mean you lack value or worth. And nothing is ever beyond repair. Until my encounter with Jesus, I did not understand how processing emotions, confessing trauma, and rising above the need for acceptance would elevate me mentally.

Rejection came in when I was too young to fight against it. In fact, back then, no one really talked about rejection and the spiritual warfare that I've learned in my adult years. This is one of the many reasons that the Bible states, "My people perish for a lack of knowledge" (Hosea 4:6). It is important that we take this knowledge to the younger generation. Most bullies themselves are dealing with rejection. Instead of giving in to those feelings they often mask them with hard-core exteriors. In dating relationships in adults, we see the same behavior. Unless people get to the roots of the rejection, they will ruin relationships by making the people who did not hurt them the object of their pain. Some examples are defensiveness, threats, manipulation, over-talking, abusive tones, and language that makes the other person feel devalued and belittled. So, you have the rejector, and the rejected. The rejected will accept these behaviors to avoid being alone, unloved, and unaccepted. The symptoms may manifest differently, but the roots remain the same. Healing rejection first starts with recognizing the point of rejection. Then the difficult work begins with destroying each branch that grew out of the root. I would suggest therapy. (A good professional Christian therapist who is able to see and hear beyond what is being said, and who can identify non-verbal cues as well).

For a man who sincerely wants his relationship to thrive, next to love, his greatest need in that relationship is respect. I know you thought I was going to say sex. While in its proper confines of marriage it is beautiful, yet its misrepresentation has been used to replace the highest love. Sex is a gift and like all of God's gifts, they can become idols. Isn't it paradoxical that what is good can also become god? Most men don't think of sex as love; its majority of women who think that way. Don't shoot the messenger, I'm speaking from my experience with women and what I've heard them verbalize. As men and women grow in God, they discover that what they once perceived as love through (sex) left them empty and ashamed. The love of God is pure, unconditional, and unequivocal to anything else. It is indescribable, and no matter how we dissect it, we are left in awe of the incredible way God loves us. This is genuine love. Going back to a man's need to be respected. Titus challenges older women to teach younger women to respect their husbands. Respect is tied to honor, which is tied to submission. It is less about control and more the need to be heralded as the head of the home. Having a mate who honors you and respects your decisions creates an atmosphere of love. I'd been disrespected in my previous marriages and relationships. That disrespect created barriers around my heart. Those walls also kept me from recognizing the fullness of God's love.

My mother was my first love. I appreciate all her sacrifices. She was very nurturing, and I will always value the lessons she taught me. I remember her telling me that she had given me to God, and I belonged to Him. I didn't know the full meaning of that then, but after coming into my own relationship with God, I understand it now. She was following the example of Hannah in the Bible who dedicated her son Samuel back to the Lord. She knew regardless of any mistakes, I'd make in life that God's hand would be ever present in my life. I recall times I didn't think he heard my prayers or even listened to them. Unknowingly, I'd reduced His love to that of those who were connected to me at the time. I perceived His love as conditional. Sure, like most church goers, I'd learned of His love for His children, and the sacrifice of Jesus on the cross, but the tiny idol of self always took center stage. I was too focused on what was missing in my life to see the beauty in what was there. While none of us are immune to rejection and or insecurities, surrendering to God will give us the mental fortitude to overcome them.

Growing up boys/men were taught not to show weakness. It has been the thorn that has destroyed many relationships;

The man and his spouse, the man and his children, and the man with himself. But weakness is where God desires us. In our weakness is where He is strongest. He beckons us to come to him as we are broken and unwalled. His love invites us to release the pain and the tears. It was God's love that gave me the courage to change and step out from the shadows of what was, into the incredible journey ahead.

THE LOVE OF GOD

God's love is unwavering and doesn't depend upon performance. He knew we'd be imperfect, and that we would stumble repeatedly. He understood that an ultimate sacrifice was needed for the forgiveness of our sins. He knew most of us wouldn't fully comprehend this love, so He sent His son, Jesus, to die for us, granting us an opportunity to receive His love and establish a relationship with Him. He provided precisely what we needed to succeed in this journey called life. No other sacrifice could have absolved the sins of the world. If love is present, its purpose is evident through actions. God's sacrifice of His son for us is the epitome of true love. Have you received it? Have you invited Jesus into your life? My friend, to succeed in life and overcome, Jesus is the only way. God's love never falters and will love you back to life. The love the world often speaks of is merely a word used carelessly, devoid of genuine intent or meaning. Love has been wielded as a tool to obtain desires, only to be discarded once satisfaction is achieved. Love is a word that surfaces when people are at their best but wanes in times of brokenness and weakness. Love diminishes when people reveal their shortcomings, and what was once seen as perfect becomes flawed. Love fades when the masks we wear to conceal our true selves are stripped away. This type of love is not what I refer to. This type of love originates from the world and offers only feelings of insecurity, pain, disappointment, brokenness, perversion, and discouragement. The world's love is never authentic and cannot yield what is true.

Embracing key truths about God's love aiding me in being liberated from rejection, abandonment, and low self-esteem. Certain religion dogma enforces rules and love according to works. It causes people to think of God with such anger and hostility toward us as humans, instead of His anger towards sin. These teachings push people away from Christ, instead of drawing them closer. We've been justified by faith. (Romans 3:28). The enemy is a master at robbing our identities in Christ. He causes us to sink under condemnation and self-judgment. He distorts the truth of righteousness so that the one thing we need, the one thing that makes us whole, and the one thing that fills every void; LOVE is tainted and obscured. The truth sets us free! "For God so loved the world that He gave His only begotten Son" (John 3:16). Throughout the Bible we see God's love wrapped in restoration and redemption. Isaiah 53:3 tells us that Christ Himself was despised and rejected. His rejection was full of our rejection. He took the pain that you and I would experience to the cross. He even faced it in His daily life. Scripture tells us that He is well acquainted with our sorrow and grief. (Hebrews 4:15)

A great sacrifice has been made for you. In fact, the reason you are alive and haven't perished in your sins is because someone gave their life for you. This individual believed you were worth every lash, every punch, every kick, every slap, every bruise, and every lie that was spoken about or against Him. The suffering didn't end with the beating; He willingly hung on a cross, shouldering the weight of your wrongdoings. This love is not comprehensible by the world, nor does it carry the same meaning. This is God's love, evident in every one of His actions towards you. The world offers a love that is fleeting and self-serving, while God extends an everlasting, life-giving love to those willing to receive it. Take a moment to contemplate the world's love and what was sacrificed for you, alongside God's love.

When you consider your life in light of the sacrifice made for you, you might wonder why. Why would someone do this for me? I have the answer to that question—it's because God loves you! I understand that right now you might be thinking that no one could possess that much love for anyone. If that's your thought, or if you believe this is mere rhetoric, I will say that you haven't fully grasped the power of love. If you genuinely comprehended what was done for you over 2000 years ago and how it remains active today, your entire perspective would change. What's lacking in that mindset is experience; we cannot adequately explain what we have not experienced. The world's love is fundamentally different from God's love, and our encounters with love cannot compare to the love God provides. Furthermore, 1 John 4:7-12 explains that we should be representatives of God's love in the earth. Apostle John wrote that we should love one another because love comes from God. We are God's children, if we share and show love. It is amazing how these foundational truths get diminished under sermons and teachings that are only focused on getting ahead, gaining wealth, and prosperity. In many cases, the focus is on "self"; Selfish motives, intentions, and desires are at the core of many podcasts and sermons.

God's love is the kind that commands love for us, and will never cease to love us, despite shortcomings, mistakes, or circumstances. No greater love than this than a man who would lay down His life for a friend. (John 15:13) This love takes the imperfect and loves it into perfection. This is real love—not that we loved God, but that he loved us and sent his Son as a sacrifice to take away our sins. (1 John 4:10)

Most of my childhood, teen, and young adult life, I misunderstood love to the extent that I pre-judged everyone as wanting something from me. I gave to gain approval and acceptance. I know the church comes under scrutiny a lot and it is true that we as an entire Body must do better in showing the love of God. That's evangelism—how can we draw them in whom we do not love? Please do not allow what you hear and see by way of imperfections and brokenness in others to turn you away from church or God. When I grew older and moved to Texas, I met a pastor who cared for my soul. He invited me to church and everyone there was full of the love of God. Pray and ask God to lead you to the place where you will know His love is real as it is demonstrated through the Body of Christ. In addition to embracing His love, we are commanded to love our neighbors as ourselves. (Mark 12:30-21)

I'd experienced love in church before, but joining my now

church home was different. The love of God was so evident, that it aided in healing the brokenness that still lingered in my soul. I knew all about sin and judgment; I'd heard those sermons my entire life; but the place God led me taught me about grace, mercy, and faith. Again, the foundational truths in the Bible must be reiterated so that the lies of the enemy are uprooted. Not only did I hear the teachings, I witnessed them firsthand through the beautiful people who spoke to me by God's spirit. I finally understood the love of God and that my future and destiny were God ordained, predestined and predetermined. Encountering God's love caused me to find my identity in Christ and find my place in His kingdom assignment. I didn't have to fit in or do things for people to accept me. I was armed with His power to combat the enemy and tear down rejection's hold over my life. Jesus took the pain and took the shame, and I accepted the beauty of His love. I didn't have to fight for attention. God is attentive because I belong to Him. You will find everything you need in God. Trust me, it's not cliche' or religious talk, it is very real. In my weakness, I found strength in God. He changed my outlook on life and gave me purpose and peace. Remember….. we love because He first loved us. (1 John 4:19) With all the choices I have had in life, and all the opportunities to seek and pursue things outside of God, I'd still choose God. I couldn't receive all of who He is, until I released all of who I was. I pray that you awaken to divine love and experience the greatest love of all.

Prayer: *Father, help me to truly understand and feel your love, so I can experience your presence in every moment of my life. Open my heart to you and let me receive your unwavering love. I am ready to embrace your love and allow it to transform my life forever. Let me be strengthened in my inner being so that Jesus will dwell richly in my heart through faith. Forgive me for self-doubt and doubting You. I repent. God, I asked that I be firmly planted and rooted in Your love so that I may be able to comprehend with all the saints the breath and length and depth of Your love..... That I be filled with the fullness of You so that no void remains in me. Let my desires be Your desires. I know You are able to do exceedingly abundantly above all that I can ask, think, or imagine, according to the glorious power of Christ Jesus that is at work in me through faith. I accept Your love and know without a doubt that I am accepted by You. I decree and declare, that I am a joint heir with Jesus Christ. I have been chosen by You from the foundation of the world. No weapon that is formed against me shall ever be able to prosper. I am more than a conqueror through Christ Jesus. I confess that I am healed from every spirit of rejection, abandonment, low self-worth, and all insecurities. My security is found in You and You alone. I am blessed with all spiritual blessings in the heavens, and I am renewed in my mind and heart. When anxious thoughts try me, in my weakness, I reply fully upon Your strength. As I surrender to You in this moment, let me see, feel, and embrace Your love that surpasses all knowledge. I love You, In Jesus' name, Amen!*

Take a moment to meditate and reflect. Write down what you feel God is speaking to you in this moment.

ABOUT THE AUTHOR

Kenneth Bonner is a devoted husband, loving father, and an ordained minister whose life is a testament to his unwavering faith and commitment to serving others. He has a B.A. in Christian Studies with an emphasis on biblical studies.

Through his love and passion for the word of God, he communicates theological truths through simple, yet impactful illustrations. His testimonies resonate with the hearts of men and women throughout the world. And he transparently shares his challenges, mistakes, struggles, and victories.

His unquenchable faith fuels his desire to bring God glory in all he does. He is filled with evangelism fire to see others saved, healed, and delivered into their destinies.

As a father of six adult children, Kenneth's familial bonds are the cornerstone of his existence. He cherishes his role to be a good steward over them. It is important to him to nurture and guide them in the admonition of the Lord, so they too can soar to greater heights in God.

To contact the author:
Email: kenneth@kennethbonnersr.com
Website: www.kennethbonnersr.com